YOUR BANK IS *RIPPING* YOU OFF

Also by Edward F. Mrkvicka, Jr.

The Rational Investor

The Bank Book

Moving Up

Battle Your Bank—and Win!

1,037 Ways to Make or Save Up to $100,000 This Year Alone

YOUR BANK IS *RIPPING* YOU OFF

Edward F. Mrkvicka, Jr.

 St. Martin's Griffin ❧ New York

332.12
MRK

Design by Pei Koay

Library of Congress Cataloging-in-Publication Data

Mrkvicka, Jr., Edward F.
    Your bank is ripping you off / by Edward F. Mrkvicka, Jr.
        p.   cm.
    ISBN 0-312-15246-9
    1. Banks and banking—Customer services—United States.
2. Banks and banking—United States.   3. Bank loans—United States.
I. Title.
HG1616.C87M743   1997   96-30824
332.1'2'0973—dc20   CIP

First St. Martin's Griffin Edition: March 1997

10   9   8   7   6   5   4   3   2   1

This book is dedicated to

the loving memory of Edward F. "Babe" Mrkvicka

Contents

Author's Note

This book offers only general banking observations based on the author's experience. It makes no specific recommendations, but was intended to provide the author's opinion in regard to subject matter.

The author and the publisher are not engaged in rendering legal or financial advice; the reader should seek the services of a qualified professional for such advice. The author and the publisher cannot be held responsible for any loss incurred as a result of the application of any of the information in this publication.

YOUR BANK IS *RIPPING* YOU OFF

Introduction

My personal research over more than twenty years indicates that you likely will overpay your bank—through mortgages, credit cards, loans, and checking and savings fees—by more than one hundred thousand dollars during your lifetime! If, instead of being cheated by your bank for all those years, you had invested that overpayment, you'd have almost ten times that amount. Whether you lost the money directly to the bank or as an investment, we're not talking about insignificant sums.

Education lets you stop your banker in his tracks; that's what this book offers. First, I am going to show you how and why the banks are ripping you off; more important, I am then going to show you how to fight back.

In 1969, I started working at a bank as a teller. By 1976, at age thirty-one, I was the chairman, president, and CEO of an Illinois national bank. I mention this for only one reason. You should judge my words by my record and the facts. Although my banking career was most successful. I left the industry because it became clear that the system was not going to change. I decided that I was at least obligated to make my knowledge available to you, the consumer, so you can better make intelligent financial decisions—decisions that may save you tens of thousands of dollars.

This is not a kiss-and-tell book. I hate it when people, who are part of a problem first milk the enterprise for all it's worth,

1

and then leave and write about how bad things were. Everything I'm going to tell you in this book I also said to my fellow bankers throughout my career. Of course, that didn't make me too popular, but I never worried about it. I was more concerned with the truth.

I believe that your bank is your financial enemy. My career experiences brought me to that conclusion. For instance, the banker who taught me about consumer loans spent half the education effort trying to convince me that customers *needed* to be abused, "so they don't cause trouble." He wanted me to make each loan customer wait a minimum of fifteen minutes before being seen, whether I was busy or not, so that I would have the upper hand in the interview. The bank deliberately designed loan applications and other forms to be difficult, if not impossible, to understand; that way, the bank would be protected in any legal dispute. And there were so many other shoddy tactics. I asked myself: Is this meeting the needs of the community? I thought not then, and I think not now. As my career progressed, it became more and more obvious that the banking system's abusive attitude toward the consumer was almost universal.

Banks are not your friends. In truth, most should be sued for false advertising. Their ads boast how much they want to help you, and yet in the back room they are deciding the best way to take as much of your money as possible.

Should any reader think I am being too hard on the industry and/or his or her bank, I ask you to reserve judgment. Read the whole text first, and then I think you'll understand my point of view. In fact, I'm betting you're going to be mad! You're going to be outraged that you've lost so much money to your "friendly" banker. You're going to realize that you've done without, or maybe you couldn't send your children to college, because you got robbed. And the robbery wasn't committed at gunpoint. It was committed by a guy or gal in a pinstriped suit sitting behind a fancy desk, who smiled all the while. To me, it doesn't matter how or why you were robbed. The result is the same. In fact, in terms of money, you're better off being robbed on the street corner. That may only cost you a couple of hundred dollars. Your banker is going to cost you tens of thousands of dollars or more!

There are good banks and bankers, but they are few and far between. If by chance you do business with an institution that cares about its community, stick with it, and support it with all your business. However, before you make that judgment, read all of this book. You may find out your "good" bank is just another bad one.

Remember, banks are your financial enemy. After you read this book, I challenge you to come to any other conclusion.

BANKING

Let's Start at the Top

To understand how your own bank is ripping you off, you need a minimal, working knowledge of how the banking industry is ripping off America. Otherwise, you will have a hard time believing that banks can get away with legally ripping off their customers; surely the government is protecting your rights, right? Let's answer that question by starting at the top with the Federal Reserve. I promise to make this lesson as quick and as painless as possible.

In 1913, Congress passed the Federal Reserve Act, which, in violation of Article I, Section 8, Clause 5 of the Constitution, gave the power to regulate money to a handful of unelected private bankers. America has been paying the price ever since.

Our Founding Fathers knew this basic truth: Those that control a nation's money control the nation. That's why they originally empowered Congress itself with the responsibility to regulate money—as, through the election process, the Constitution gave ultimate authority for our currency where it was intended—to voters, the people. Nevertheless, after extensive lobbying by some of the most powerful and wealthy bankers of the day, the passage of the Federal Reserve Act handed our economic future to an unsupervised private corporation called the Federal Reserve.

The Fed is worthy of review for many reasons, the most pressing being our over five-trillion-dollar national debt. This intolerable, crushing financial obligation threatens our country's very existence. And a prime force that has brought us to the edge of the insolvency abyss is the Federal Reserve Act and the Federal Reserve itself.

As the Federal Reserve is a private banking institution, every time Congress requisitions money it creates a debt obligation. There have been thousands of these monetary transactions since 1913, in which a transfer of cash from the Fed is made in exchange for U.S. Bonds. This results in taxpayers' paying untold billions of dollars in interest every year, with no hope of reducing the principal. By controlling our money, private Federal Reserve bankers have indebted us all, forever. That's the nature of the Federal Reserve Act money/debt structure.

Here's a thought: A government that prints its own money shouldn't be indebted. So why is ours? The Federal Reserve is the unfortunate answer. That's why we don't have a truly free economy. Government, instead of using our hard-earned tax dollars to pay for needed housing, education, mass transit, health care, and other critical social services, pays interest on the national debt—a debt due in large part to the Federal Reserve, a bank owned solely by America's commercial banks. If we eliminated the Federal Reserve middleman, we would be able to create a debt-free government productive at all levels.

The Fed is so powerful that not even the president can sit in on its secret meetings to set interest rates. Congress and the Supreme Court too are virtually powerless when it comes to the Federal Reserve. It is monetarily omnipotent.

The Fed is supposed to be independent, but everyone knows that's not the case. Historically, the Federal Reserve Board has set policy according to what's best for the banking industry, not what's best for the consumer. The consumer's interests are, at best, ignored. Even the economy takes a backseat, unless the bankers' interests happen to coincide with what's best for the economy. That's how it works. Why? Once again, because the Fed is owned by its member banks. That's why it's not "independent." The fox is guarding the henhouse.

How does the Fed affect you at your own bank? Let me give you one quick example. When the Federal Reserve Board of Governors meets to set the Fed fund interest rate (the interest rate the Fed charges member banks to borrow money), the entire interest-rate structure of the country is in turn affected. If the Fed increases its interest rate, all business and consumer rates go up, usually by a like or additional amount. That's how you're affected. If the Fed says so, you'll pay more for your mortgage, your car loan, and so on.

A final thought on this topic in the form of a rhetorical question, which I'll answer myself: How can an economy be free if interest rates are set behind closed doors at the Federal Reserve? It can't.

The United States, while not the economic power it once was, is still the richest nation in the world. Yet average Americans possess virtually none of this wealth. Thomas Jefferson was prophetic when he stated, "If the American people ever allow private banks to control the issue of their currency, first by inflation and then by deflation, the banks and the corporations that will grow up around them will deprive the people of all property until their children wake up homeless on the continent their fathers conquered."

Without overstating to make a point, the Federal Reserve is a tool of economic totalitarianism. It has allowed a small number of private bankers to enslave America financially. And if they can do that, they can do almost anything.

Competition? No, Collusion

The banker's definition of the prime lending rate is "that interest rate the banks charge their best commercial customers."

All other interest rates are by design connected to prime. If prime is at X percent, mortgages are at X plus percent, personal installment loans at "X" plus, plus percent, and so on. At face value, it would seem logical for the banks to have a baseline for their lending policies and rates. Certainly the country's financial markets have come to accept the banker's premise in terms of prime. The concept of prime has never been challenged. No one questions or attempts to negotiate his loan interest rate downward as long as that rate has some reasonable relationship to the prime rate. In fact, most of us, including major corporate borrowers, feel we have a bargain if we are allowed to borrow at one or two percentage points above prime.

Financial institutions have, for their own purposes, created this public misconception about the prime lending rate. That misconception, more than any other, costs consumers billions in added interest expense each and every year.

The misconception is that there really is any such thing as a prime lending rate. There is no such rate, never has been, and never will be. It is a concoction of the financial institutions' community that allows banks to charge interest rates far in excess of a fair rate that can be justified by cost analysis.

Bankers, when trying to define prime, will tell you it's derived from a complicated formula that takes into account the bank's cost of money (the interest it pays on deposits), associated business expenses (such as salaries and office space, and so on). They will go to great lengths to explain that prime is set within a competitive environment with related market forces coming into play. Of course, all of this is nonsense.

If interest rates are, in fact, a reflection of the market, then each bank's cost of money should be different from that of its competition. It should be obvious that the cost of money for a bank in rural Illinois is different than that of a major money-center bank in New York City, as the cost of acquiring and maintaining an account will vary.

Salary expense (a bank's second-largest expense after interest costs) most assuredly will differ. For example, bank employees in New Mexico, on average, make less than those in Los Angeles.

It is even clearer that office or plant costs vary, as some banks are housed in fifty-story monuments while others rent storefronts in small rural communities.

Bankers will mention other factors in the fixing of prime, but these are the major considerations. I mention them to make evident that, assuming there were such a thing as prime (the banker's definition), each bank would have to have a formula that would yield a different rate than that for all other banks. "Prime" might have some parameters, but it would be a range rather than a set figure—and in some cases the variance would be quite large. In an ideal environment, the customer would be able to shop for the best deal.

The banker's formula starts to fall apart at the bottom line. That line says that if prime were real in a competitive sense, there would be as many different prime lending rates as there are banks. Yet, prime is the same in Boston as it is in Los Angeles, as it is in Miami, as it is in Alaska. This is the same as price fixing. Financial institutions championed deregulation on the premise that the market itself was better able to set interest rates, and that added competition would be beneficial to the consumer. However, prime is set in a completely closed environment. There is no rate competition. There is no consumer benefit.

Bankers know that as long as Fed bankers control the Fed fund rate and they themselves control prime, they control the market. The facade of deregulation and its associated "consumer benefits" has become so transparent it is an embarrassment to the financial industry. A monopoly by any other name is still a monopoly.

Interest rates are always artificially high because of prime and the way it is set. Money is always tighter than it should be for the same reason. There is an unspoken, yet clearly visible, conspiracy to deny consumers their right to financial comparison shopping.

Exactly how does this prime control take place? Very simply, prime is set by a handful of major money-center banks, again with no competition, and everyone else follows them. Each money-center bank has hundreds of correspondent banks (banks that have a mutual account relationship) that call its money desk each morning to ask what the prime rate is for the day. Then the correspondent bank moves its prime rate according to what rate the money-center bank has set. As you can imagine, since most larger banks have inherently higher costs than their smaller hometown correspondents, their prime rate will always be higher than what the correspondents' prime should be, based on cost analysis. Yet, they have the same prime rate. Why? Because those community banks stand to make additional profit by using the inflated prime rate of their larger correspondent bank. When you remember that even the money-center banks create prime out of thin air, this passing on of rate becomes even more ludicrous.

With prime, in addition to its deceptiveness and its added cost to the consumer, there is another consideration. Setting prime in this way violates the interpretive rulings of the comptroller of the currency, administrator of national banks. Specifically, Interpretive Ruling 7.800 states, "Charges by banks (a) All charges to customer should be arrived at by each bank on a competitive basis and not on the basis of any agreement, arrangement, undertaking, understanding or discussion with any other banks or their officers." No discussion! There are discussions every morning for the sole purpose of establishing a universal prime lending rate.

If this is true, then why hasn't the government stepped in and ended this unabashed price fixing? The government doesn't enforce its own rules and regulations because the government needs the banks more than it needs the approval of the financial consumer. You see, you can't finance two-hundred-billion-dollar yearly budget shortfalls by selling twenty-five-dollar savings bonds. You have to sell million-dollar bond issues. And who has that capability? The banks. Banks have become the conduit from our checking and savings accounts to the Federal Treasury. Without this banking lifeline, the government would have to admit it is bankrupt, and/or start printing more and more fiat money (money that must be accepted as legal tender but is not backed by any hard asset, such as gold or silver) to pay the national debt now exceeding five trillion dollars.

The government will do nothing to protect the financial consumer. Forget what the law says. Judge government's intentions not by words, but by deeds. The government has done nothing to stop bankers from price fixing interest rates (and service charges). In fact, it sanctifies it.

More Competition? No, More Collusion

Deregulation, approved by Congress in the 1980s at the insistence of major money-center banks, was heralded as the Second Coming for bank consumers. Now, for the first time, depositors were to receive interest on their checking-account balances, and there would be free-market competition among banks for our savings dollars. It was anticipated that competition would help increase savings rates across the board. Competition was also supposed to free up money for housing starts, mortgages, small-business lending, and so on. It was with this consumer-benefit thrust that banks championed deregulation.

Big banks spent time and money convincing Congress that deregulation was in the best interest of those the legislators represented. All banks, once deregulation became a reality, spent additional time and money convincing the public that their needs could be better served by allowing the market to dictate their cost of money. To be fair, deregulation did hold such promise, yet there were many of us in the industry who had grave reservations.

Immediately, bankers' motives were suspect, despite their seemingly altruistic touting of consumer interests. The timing of deregulation makes clear the bankers' true intentions, as it was implemented at a time when industry excesses were indicating that banking was in jeopardy. Unfortunately, it was in this fertile field that the seeds of deregulation were sown. It should have been apparent that an industry already malfunctioning in a virtually nonaccountable environment would not fare any better left completely to its own devices. (Banks are highly regulated, but enforcement is minimal—then too, even when violations are found, there is seldom a penalty to the offending institution.) Banks had decided to pass the burden of responsibility for their own performance and destiny to the consumer; deregulation was the perfect means to that end.

Over and above industry concerns, there were other, more important consumer considerations in the move to deregulation. Notwithstanding the promise of some deregulation, certain facts became obvious. While it is true that checking-account balances could now receive interest, it is also true that for most accounts added service charges more than offset the income. In fact, most consumers are paying far more for bank services than ever before. Despite the moral imperative of their banking charters, many bankers used deregulation to price their services out of the reach of many customers they are supposed to serve. Bankers believe the most profitable combination is higher costs to fewer customers.

It should have occurred to Congress that it was being sold a bill of goods, as common sense dictates the average family owes more than it has saved. Therefore, while competitive interest rates in the savings arena might have a positive effect on a few people, the associated rise in lending interest rates would have a negative effect on most. And this observation ignores the attendant increase in service charges. The net effect of deregulation to the banks has been record profits. The net effect to the consumer has been less personal, more costly service. I hammer on this point because it's so important.

The bottom line here is: Banks advocated deregulation as a consumer benefit, and then, once it was approved by a malleable Congress, repackaged as many services as possible to isolate the industry from any exposure that deregulated free-market forces might bring. They effectively flipped a coin and called heads—and tails—simultaneously.

There is one more important result of the banks' collusion in deregulation. It was a major factor in the collapse of the savings-and-loan industry; it cost taxpayers untold billions. Bankers knew this would be the result of deregulation; in fact, that was part of the plan.

Deregulation opened up "competition" for the savings dollar. That was a competition that the S&Ls would surely lose, because, unlike banks, they had virtually all of their assets invested in long-term, fixed-rate mortgages. So when deregulation temporarily raised savings rates, the S&Ls saw their profit margin disappear. (I say temporarily, because once the S&Ls were gutted, savings rates plummeted to approximately half of what they were prior to deregulation.) Deregulation turned many profitable S&Ls into part of the taxpayer bailout. Again, sadly, that was part of the bankers' plan. Bankers got to kill two birds with one stone. Deregulation gave them more opportunity to increase profits from customers, while providing less service and reducing competition. In some cases, banks bought up the remains of some S&Ls. What a windfall! No, that isn't quite accurate, because a windfall is happenstance—this was collusion.

Screw the Consumer, Let's Go Where the Profit Is

Foreign debt, once so profitable to private U.S. banks, has become a pressing, national economic problem. In fact, the delinquency of most of our debtors may someday be the catalyst that ignites a nationwide banking catastrophe.

The taxpayer has been forced to subsidize the income of those banks that extended this imprudent credit, as the United States is the principal contributor to both the World Bank and International Monetary Fund, which is where delinquent countries borrow additional monies to pay the banks their past-due interest. Without this taxpayer assistance, many major banks would be forced to close. That's as it should be. Unsound banks, like other mismanaged businesses, should close in a true free market. However, the American Banker's Association has lobbied long and hard for involuntary financial support from taxpayers, and the additional tax breaks that Congress has so willingly given time and time again. Is it possible that Congress and the ABA don't actually believe in a free market?

It should also be noted that shareholders of banks that have substantial delinquent foreign debt are being deluded. By allowing the banks to carry these past-due foreign loans as earning assets, the Federal Deposit Insurance Corporation (FDIC), the comptroller of the currency, and state banking agencies have encouraged the industry deception of creative bookkeeping. Thus a bank that may present itself as a profitable, stable institution might in fact be failing, and shareholders could see their investment lost while never understanding why. The fact is, if delinquent foreign debt were charged-off in the same ways as other nonperforming assets (loans)—which is what are—a number of major money-center banks would be forced to close immediately.

A more important problem is the hidden cost of foreign debt. That foreign debt, approximately a trillion dollars, was subtracted from the available lending pool, which tightened money. It was removed from our lending pool because bankers could get a much better return in interest, service charges, and loan fees abroad than they could get from the American consumer. So what if they are using our money? This increased your, the consumer's, cost of money regardless of whether your bank has foreign debtors. Instead of leaving the country, this money should have been used to finance American business expansion, new-car purchases, home mortgages, college educations. But, because the banks earned more profit from foreign debt than our market would supply, the money left the country. In so doing, I would argue, the banks have violated the intent of the Community Reinvestment Act (CRA) of 1977. The CRA states that regulated financial institutions are required by law to demonstrate that their deposit facilities (credit as well as deposit services) serve the convenience and needs of the communities in which they are chartered to do business.

Most financial experts agree that if the money loaned to foreign debt or nations had not left the country, loan rates—regardless of where they are at the moment—would be lowered by one to three percentage points. Let's use the lowest figure. That extra one percentage point means a $10,000 car loan (forty-eight-month term) costs the consumer an additional $400, due to foreign debt. A home mortgage of $100,000 (thirty-year amortization) costs an additional $70 per month, $840 per year, and $25,200 to complete term, due to foreign debt. And these are just two examples. Imagine the total additional cost for the millions of bank loans made throughout the year. Imagine the total cost if we used the three percentage-point figure!

As a conservative free-market advocate I abhor government intervention. However, the facts (and bankers' misjudgments) are clear. The consumer deserves protection from present and future foreign-debt abuses. If the Congress cannot bring itself to act on behalf of the personal finances of the electorate it should be convinced on the basis of the preservation of the banking industry itself.

While creative bookkeeping and burying our legislative heads in the sand may seem to solve the problem in the present, it does nothing concrete. The foreign-debt crisis can no longer be ignored. Even the much-heralded Mexican debt-restructuring program was woefully inadequate, akin to offering Band-Aids and aspirin to a cancer patient. If that wasn't the case, why the 1995 Mexican bailout?

More important, the popularity of foreign debt is more proof of the fact that banks no longer care about their local communities.

Too Many Banks Don't Like Women, Blacks, and Other Minorities

"The Federal Equal Credit Opportunity Act prohibits creditors from discriminating against applicants on the basis of race, color, religion, national origin, sex, marital status, age (provided the applicant has the capacity to enter into a binding contract); because all or part of the applicants' income derives from any public assistance; or because the applicant has in good faith exercised any right under the Consumer Credit Protection Act."

This is the notice that banks include on their credit applications. It could be assumed then they understand that financial discrimination is illegal. Logic dictates, therefore, that discrimination should no longer be a problem for the banking consumer.

Nothing could be further from the truth. Banks practice financial discrimination each and every business day.

For the purpose of this section we will review how discrimination affects lending. There are, of course, other arenas in which individuals or groups feel the harsh results of financial discrimination, but it has made its hardest impact here.

The Equal Credit Opportunity Act (ECOA) was made necessary by the historical abuses of the banking industry. In most cases Congress has rubber-stamped whatever the bankers want. In the case of financial discrimination, the abuses were so apparent and/or racially motivated that Congress was forced by public demand to act. Congress was then faced with addressing the issue without actually doing anything of substance. Hence was born the ECOA, congressional cosmetics at their worst. It placated the consumer groups that were demanding action for banking discrimination, while giving no actual relief to those so abused.

Congress then charged the Federal Trade Commission (FTC) with administering ECOA compliance. The commission has been embarrassingly weak in using its authority against financial institutions that even now continually generate complaints of discrimination. My research makes clear that the ECOA has very little, if any, merit for the consumer. It looks good. Unfortunately, that's all it does.

The proof is on the record. There are more financial-discrimination complaints on record than ever before, and yet actions against individual banks by banking agencies (the comptroller of the currency, the *FDIC,* and state banking authorities) are virtually nonexistent. Actions against banks by the FTC are equally scarce. Congress didn't solve the financial-discrimination problem; it gave the banks an Act to hide behind instead.

For those of you who have never suffered financial discrimination, this may have little meaning. Others understand personally why I am addressing the issue. Financial discrimination can be the worst discrimination of all, for its ramifications are endless. Often, the discrimination of one bank can affect the relationship you have with another bank. If discrimination becomes a matter affecting your credit report, it can destroy a financial lifetime.

Discrimination by financial institutions and others that extend credit is easy to understand. Loan officers are only human, and as such are subject to imperfections and subjectivity that can adversely affect others. Good loan officers, of which there are all too few, realize their limitations and bend over backwards to be reasonable toward marginal credit applications, especially if the application is from someone they do not like. Some loan officers will give the application to another officer to make the final judgment, ensuring that the consumer gets a fair answer. Unfortunately these loan officers are rare. Most simply fall prey to their prejudices and pass them on to the applicant, by turning down the loan out of hand.

Of course, your credit denial will never reflect that discrimination. No loan officer in his right mind will ever admit discrimination, especially in writing! The credit-denial form lists many reasons that can be checked off to explain why you were denied. All the officer need do is find one that remotely fits your circumstances. He knows no federal agency is ever going to pursue the matter with him personally. The wording of the ECOA virtually assures that. The Act calls for the loan officer to supply written notice indicating why you were denied credit. Does the Federal Trade Commission think that a loan officer is going to admit, "you were denied credit because you're black [a woman, Jewish, whatever]"? Since the Act's inception there have been tens of millions of credit denials. In all my research, and that of various other consumer groups, not one credit denial has indicated overt discrimination! That record represents either the most remarkable altruism in the history of mankind, or indicates the whole process is a sham.

The banking industry's unwillingness to obey the law was reported in a *Chicago Tribune* article a few short years ago, headlined, "Mortgage Study Finds Bias Beneath Excuses."

The article stated that the "one-year investigation . . . concludes that, all other factors being equal, black and Hispanic mortgage applicants are roughly 60 percent more likely to be denied a loan than whites." The report quoted another study that used the 1991 statistics from the Home Mortgage Disclosure Act, which concluded, "black applicants were rejected twice as often as whites for mortgages."

In effect, even the Civil Rights Act is being misused by the banking industry.

Something else came to light during my research for this book. I state without fear of being proven wrong that financial institutions routinely practice discrimination. In fairness, for a while it seemed like racial discrimination had decreased. Times changed, and the area receiving the most benefit from this attitude shift was financial discrimination against minorities. Banks, having been forced by law to finance minority businesses, forced to stop *redlining*, suddenly realized that the ethnic groups that they had been avoiding pay their bills too. These people were no better or worse than anyone else. The Civil Rights Act made its most unnoticed, yet powerful contribution in the financial marketplace. Specifically, many ethnic groups suddenly had access to credit for the first time. Their ability to handle that responsibility forever put to rest any basis for the denial of credit based on race. Or did it?

Here are some additional quotes from a 1995 article in the *Chicago Tribune*:

> Northern [Trust], the nation's 35th-largest financial institution, agreed to establish a $700,000 fund, rather than pay a fine, to compensate at least 63 African-American and Hispanic families denied home mortgages in 1992 and 1993.
>
> The Justice Department said the denials occurred because of a pattern of discrimination that resulted in "significant difference" in the treatment of white and minority applicants.
>
> "In [the] Northern Trust case, the Justice Department charged that Northern loan officers used different standards to evaluate loan applications from whites than those used to evaluate minority applications."

Sorry, folks, banks continue to violate the law. Some readers may be thinking, Doesn't this prove that the government is properly overseeing the industry? My answer is a resounding, No! Again, racial discrimination is a subject that the government has been unable to ignore as it pertains to banks. It is a politically explosive issue. But notice which agency is taking action: the Department of Justice—not the FDIC, the comptroller of the currency, the state baking agencies, or the Federal Reserve. No, all the agencies that should be taking action are using their resources to try to stop such actions by the Justice Department. Don't be fooled and think that government regulation has solved the problem.

Sadly, not only are banks guilty of racial discrimination, they have expanded their discrimination base to include three new categories: women, the young, and the elderly.

Women are discriminated against for all the predictable reasons. First, most loan officers are men. As such, they have difficulty assessing the creditworthiness of the opposite sex in an objective manner. Some men aren't comfortable with women in the business world. Others don't believe women of childbearing age will be able to make their loan payments because "what happens if she gets pregnant"? Still other men don't like women to get ahead, especially ahead of *them*, so they deny them business credit.

Young credit applicants are usually denied credit because many banks have little foresight. That is to say, they don't want to be the first one to loan money to the untested. They want you to establish your credit rating before applying to them. The ludicrousness of that Catch-22 deserves no further comment.

Elderly applicants are often shocked to find that years of maintaining quality bank accounts with an institution count for very little when they apply for a loan. Banks don't want the hassle of collecting from the elderly if they become sick and/or disabled. Nor do they want to wait for the estate to be settled in case of death. To the point, they want your deposits, they don't want your loan business.

The fact is, although banks have shifted their discrimination focus somewhat and have become more adept at hiding their transgressions, they are still in the business of denying credit to applicants based on one or more of the aspects prohibited by the ECOA. They will not be above board with their actions, but when you strip away all the tinsel, they're guilty.

The Capital Con

Can you name one service that your bank offers that you cannot acquire elsewhere at a reduced cost? I have yet to meet a banker who can answer that question. You can establish a checking account through numerous other avenues such as a credit union or brokerage house. You can borrow money from private outlets at a reduced rate. You can save money with private individuals or corporate firms at a greater return. There are safe deposit and trust companies, consulting firms, and so on available to you.

By themselves banks serve no purpose. What other corporate entity makes the customer pay for the on-the-shelf product? Compare a bank to any retail store. Do the patrons of the store have to pay for the shelf stock before they purchase the same merchandise at the retail level? Of course not, yet that's what bank consumers must do. They deposit money (stock the shelves) so they can purchase the same product (money). Even bankers would have to admit they are part of a unique business. They have the best of both worlds. Retail stores make 100 percent investment in merchandise before they even open their doors. Banks don't. They have little investment. Typically a bank's capital-to-asset ratio is 7 percent; unfortunately, many banks are below even this minuscule percentage, and yet they are big business. How? They use other people's money. Banks are nothing more than middlemen. They are, judging by every generally accepted business practice and ratio, grossly undercapitalized. Therefore, because of their capital structure and resource allocation, even the most healthy are subject to immediate collapse.

Banks hold in their own cash reserves only a small portion of the bank's total deposits. Even totalling their investments that might be termed liquid—immediately salable loans, bonds, and so on—doesn't help. Why the small liquidity? The industry is designed to place most of its investments in high-return loans—consumer loans, car loans, mortgages, and so on—loans that cannot quickly be turned into cash under normal circumstances. Most banks are at least 75 percent "loaned out," so they possess only a small portion of assets that might be turned into cash.

Consequently, however "strong" or "profitable" the bank, if enough depositors on any given day wish to withdraw all their money, the bank cannot comply. The bank, in effect, would be closed. Without consumer confidence any bank can shut down, the strength of its financial statement notwithstanding. This precarious capital flaw was designed by greedy bankers. And they perpetuate this system by lobbying strenuously every time someone suggests substantially raising the banking industry's capital structure, or adding regulations that would better protect the consumer's money and rights. They want to take only limited risk with their capital. Our deposits are another matter. The point is, every bank, and therefore the entire banking industry, is an exceptionally fragile business entity. Does this fact give credibility to the bankers' argument that they need a veil of secrecy to protect against the destruction of consumer confidence? Quite the contrary. As the system is so (intentionally) fragile, shareholders and depositors are entitled to know the true status of their bank. How else can they protect their investments or deposits?

This subject wasn't critical when the banking system was stable, but current events make clear it no longer is. It's in a state of looming crisis that makes an understanding of banking's capital deficiency mandatory. The inner workings of the business demonstrate that a Depression-type problem—a "run" on banks, where unstable economic conditions cause customers to withdraw their savings—is possible even under the best of circumstances. In today's climate it becomes all too conceivable.

Without adequate capital, the only people to lose when a bank closes, or worse yet, in a national banking collapse, will be shareholders, depositors, and taxpayers. The bankers have virtually nothing of their own invested, and therefore nothing to lose. This is one of the lessons that should have been learned from the S&L collapse.

Bankers Want More Freedom—to Pillage

In 1929 the stock market crashed. That was the precursor to the Great Depression.

In 1932 Senate hearings concluded that large money-center banks had used questionable, and possibly illegal, tactics in order to underwrite issues of stocks and bonds. Further, they determined that the banks' entry into this highly speculative investment form was in great part responsible for the crash of 1929. The final result of the hearing was the Glass-Steagall Act, which prohibits commercial banks from corporate underwriting.

Glass-Steagall has stood this country well, yet is now under substantial pressure from banking lobbyists. Their motivation is, as always, profits. Faced with the very real possibility of Third World debt losses, and the present loss of a large portion of the savings dollar to the better interest rates being offered on Wall Street and in the corporate sector, banks want once again to enter the exceptionally profitable and highly volatile arena of stock and bond underwriting.

In their presentations to Congress, bankers are using quotes from such financial notables as former Fed chairman Paul Volcker, who wrote, "I believe legislation should be adopted promptly to give straightforward authority for bank holding companies to engage in certain underwriting activities." As hard as it is to fathom, even after the "Crash of '87," the current Fed chairman, Alan Greenspan, has taken the same position.

Volcker, Greenspan, and the bankers are wrong. Giving banks the ability to underwrite speculative issues is to risk once again a general economic crisis. The bankers of today are no more intelligent than or morally superior to the bankers of 1929. Therefore it is not inconceivable that the end result would be the same, or worse.

Let's remember that banks have been given a legislative monopoly based, in part, on the fact that they typically invest in relatively secure financial vehicles. By design, they are the country's major financial provider of consumer services, and as such have been allowed unprecedented concessions to enhance their profit base. Allowing their reentry into underwriting would give them an edge in an already unlevel financial playing field. The last time the banks had the best of both worlds, the stock market collapsed. Glass-Steagall has for more than sixty years protected the banks from the bankers, and there is no logical reason to reverse the Act's positive results.

There are other aspects of the banker's lobby that need to be addressed. Underwriting by banks could be used to repackage nonperforming bank loans into securities that could then be sold to the unsuspecting public. That very circumstance happened in the 1920s, so it is not farfetched to fear a recurrence. Then there is the possibility that the banks will start intermingling their underwriting funds with the consumer deposits that the government insures. This too is a logical concern, since many bankers have recently been found guilty of illegal insider transactions. It seems likely that the extremely profitable underwriting would at some point be compromised by the industry's desire for additional profits. Should that scenario occur, we would face a ludicrous situation in which the government in effect insures the most highly speculative investments. This fail-safe position would encourage the banks to take even greater risks, as recent history has shown that the government will not allow a major money-center bank to close.

Congress should not be pressured to repeal Glass-Steagall and/or give the banks any additional rights to enter additional markets, such as insurance or real estate. The historical record of the banking industry makes clear that, to protect the consumer, banks need additional supervision, not less. They have made a mess of the market they are supposed to serve on more than one occasion. They shouldn't be turned loose to spread their failures once again. Common sense dictates that commercial bankers and their hometown capital, deposits, and loans don't belong on Wall Street. History taught us a most valuable lesson in 1929. Bankers are hoping you've forgotten.

The Best Way to "Rob" a Bank Is to Work for One

Most would agree that when someone excels at his or her job, that person deserves to be rewarded. That's the bottom line of the American work ethic.

That philosophy pertains not only to the individual, but to an industry as well. An industry's reward culminates in that industry's growth, which usually brings more profits. Those profits are then passed on to shareholders, and (theoretically) to employees.

Reward: That's what most of us strive for, on both a personal and professional level.

Sometimes, however, outcomes don't seem to make sense. A case in point is the banking industry. The banking industry is playing by a different set of rules—rules that are gouging money from your future.

I believe no one should be adverse to paying for expertise in any field. This is probably more true in the area of finance than most. So, if the banking industry is performing well, it has a right to prosper (within the confines of being a government-sanctioned monopoly), and so do bank employees. Yet, herein lies the iniquity.

Recent salary survey reports indicate that only 2 percent of American households are headed by persons who work in the banking and other financial fields. Yet these individuals own 31 percent of the nation's wealth! Further, their yearly income is substantially skewed in relation to their proportion in the population. With salaries in the $150,000.00 to $279,999.00 range, this 2 percent represents a staggering 17 percent slice of the income pie. (I am talking about bank officers and directors here. Bank line employees are typically grossly underpaid.) Clearly, top bankers are well paid. The question is, how and why?

I can tell you the how quite succinctly. They overcharge their customers! And things are getting worse. Since deregulation, banks have raised their service charges as much as 400 percent.

The "why" is impossible to rationalize. Based on industry performance, bankers should be making moderate salaries at best. But, that's what the banking system is all about; it's designed *by* bankers *for* bankers. The disproportionate figures allow for no other conclusion.

I bring these facts to your attention for more than shock value: I want to make it clear that you must be careful where you bank. You, and you alone, have to isolate your finances from those in the banking industry who are using the system solely for their own gain.

Bankers live the good life, no matter how incompetent they may be. If their bank is poorly run and not profitable, they simply raise account service charges, charge higher interest rates for loans. They never cut their own salaries. Even if the bank fails and is closed, the government steps in and protects the bankers, often ensuring that their expensive "golden parachutes" are paid (while shareholders, and perhaps even creditors often aren't) despite that it was management that was solely responsible for the bank's collapse.

Bankers have a good deal going. You're paying for it—and it's a disgrace.

Deceive, Deceive, Deceive

Banks make much of their income by deceiving customers. They withhold information that would allow you to make intelligent financial decisions. One example of this evasion involves credit life and disability insurance, a topic we'll cover later. Another excellent example is the language used on loan agreements. That's what I'll use here to show you how underhanded the industry—and your bank—can be.

Bankers know that few borrowers bother to read the fine print of a loan agreement. You trust your banker, and/or you know there is little chance of deciphering the bank legalese. Your banker, of course, doesn't want you to read and understand the technicalities of your obligation. That should give you pause to reevaluate your banking relationship. Entering into an agreement that you don't understand is bad enough. Doing so because the other party, in this case your bank, has made every effort to ensure you can't is quite another thing. The wording of loan agreements is a flagrant example of your bank's continuing effort to put you and your family at a disadvantage.

Lest you think I am exaggerating, let's review a few standard loan clauses typically included in bank lending contracts.

BANK LEGALESE: "To guarantee payment hereof, the undersigned jointly and severally irrevocably authorize any attorney or court of record to appear for any one or more of them in such court in term or vacation, after default in payment hereof and confess a judgment without process in favor of the creditor hereof for such an amount as may appear unpaid."

INTERPRETATION: If the bank decides to sue because of a delinquency, you've agreed to let them win even if you had a perfectly valid reason for not paying. Believe it or not, you've also agreed to the obvious ethical conflict of having the bank's attorney represent both you and the bank in court.

BANK LEGALESE: "Each of us individually and severally waives any and all benefit or relief from all exemptions or moratoriums to which the signers or any of them may be entitled under the laws of this or any other state now in force or hereafter passed against this debt."

INTERPRETATION: If you are in default, you have given the bank the right to take property that, without this waiver, would have been protected from seizure.

BANK LEGALESE: "We severally authorize and direct our employers or future employers to pay a part of our salary, wages, commissions, or other compensation for services to the said assignee and release such employers or any future employers from all liability to us on account of any and all monies paid in accordance with the terms hereof. We severally give and grant unto the said assignee full power and authority to demand, receive, and receipt for the same of any part thereof in any of our names."

INTERPRETATION: If you are delinquent, you have given the bank the right to demand immediately a portion of your salary to satisfy their debt. You will not argue about it regardless of the circumstances.

BANK LEGALESE: "If this agreement is referred to any attorney for collection due to default or breach of any promise or provision hereunder by debtor, debtor agrees to pay reasonable attorney fees plus court costs."

INTERPRETATION: If the bank sues, you've agreed to pay *their* lawyer.

BANK LEGALESE: "Default in the payment of any installment of the principal or charges hereof or any part of either shall, at the option of the holder hereof, render the entire balance, principal and interest, at once due and payable."

INTERPRETATION: If you miss a single monthly payment, the bank can call the whole loan due immediately.

BANK LEGALESE: "The undersigned jointly and severally agree that the lender may communicate with any persons whatsoever in relation to this obligation involved, or its delinquency, in an effort to obtain cooperation to help relative to the collection or payment thereof."

INTERPRETATION: If you are delinquent, the bank can tell your friends and relatives.

These clauses may or may not be used by your bank. However, they are fairly common, and represent only a small sample of the many potentially damaging clauses used on varying loan contracts.

My point: There is probably no greater credit pitfall you can make than signing a loan that waives virtually all your rights as a credit consumer. Yet, almost all banks do everything they can to ensure that's exactly what you do. Sadly, they are not even above board in these tactics. They use the fine print and bank legalese in the hope you will never realize, until it's too late, that you've little or no recourse in a loan dispute.

This one example should serve to caution you that the bank, an institution that advertises itself as your friend, is, judging from its dubious loan contracts, exactly the opposite.

Our Safety Net Has a Big Hole in It

The Federal Deposit Insurance Corporation (FDIC) is an independent executive agency formed to insure deposits of all banks entitled to their insurance coverage. Its performance, until recently, has been adequate, and most consumers have come to rely on its financial assurance that all deposits will be returned to their rightful owners regardless of the fate of the bank in which they reside.

While it has long been known that the FDIC's monetary reserves were pitifully small when compared to the sum of the deposits it was insuring, it was also fairly acknowledged that those reserves were acceptable based on the small number of actual forced bank closings, coupled with the number of institutions under forced government supervision. Since the Depression, bank closings have normally been fewer than twenty per year. Banks on the FDIC problem list—the list comprised of institutions one step away from being closed—have usually been fewer than two hundred. In this financial climate, it was of little concern that the FDIC reserve paled next to the deposits it insured. But, times have changed (see Appendix charts A and B); the number of unstable banks has dramatically increased.

Although the last few years have seen a noticeable improvement in industry strength (improved profits), there is still cause for concern, because the improvement is attributable almost entirely to the aberrational large rate spread between savings and loan rates. Without that and outrageous bank fees, banks would have continued to close at a record rate. Unfortunately, bankers didn't take advantage of the engineered "happenstance" and didn't retool the industry to prevent this from happening again. It's still business as usual. Bankers learned nothing from the S&L collapse, and the attendant record bank closings between 1982 and 1992. Why does this environment of potential collapse still exist? Because of a consistent pattern of government neglect and banker abuse.

For many years, beginning in 1981, bank closings and the problem list were growing at record rates that should have alerted all appropriate government agencies that something was amiss. Yet, the FDIC did little to shore up its reserves to meet the added risk exposure. Finally, by 1991, the FDIC—your deposit safety net—was in the red by seven billion dollars. That, folks, is malfeasance.

Using the Federal Savings and Loan Association (FSLIC) as a model, deep concern about the FDIC's fate becomes inevitable. While the specifics vary, there is an important parallel. Due to the S&L bailout, the FSLIC saw its reserves disappear; in effect, it went bankrupt and closed down, costing taxpayers billions and billions of dollars. While the FDIC reserves have grown since the 1991 depletion, the policies that saw them go into the red are still in place, meaning they could end up depleted once again.

The failed Ohio deposit-insurance program provides an example of the road the FDIC is traveling. At the time it collapsed, the state of Ohio plan had reserves (as compared to deposits) equal to any held by the FDIC in recent memory, yet still it collapsed because, like the FDIC, it only carried a small reserve of the deposits it "insured." The same occurred in the banking crises of Maryland and Rhode Island a few year ago. These historical precedents cannot be ignored.

As a defensive maneuver, administrators of the FDIC have repeatedly reassured the public that their agency is backed "by the full faith and credit of the federal government." While that fact is philosophically soothing, it means next to nothing, as the federal government itself is running annual deficits of approximately two hundred billion dollars, which is then added to our five-trillion-dollar national debt. Applying the lending standards of the banking industry itself, the government's guarantee can no longer seriously be considered viable.

The FDIC has additional problems. In order to avoid closing those large money-center banks that are insolvent—and therefore expose the limits of its own reserves—the FDIC has had to nationalize a segment of the financial "free market," as it did with Continental Illinois National Bank. In the future, that policy may have to be employed repeatedly because a staggering number of major banks now have financial vulnerabilities. That means the FDIC could be the owner of the very banks it is supposed to supervise. That is an unacceptable conflict of interest, for it accelerates the consumers' and taxpayers' risk.

From my point of view, the FDIC has already failed in principle. That principle doesn't have to evolve into fact. But until the banking industry starts policing its ranks, bank closings are reduced to close to zero, the "problem list" shrinks to a handful of institutions, and FDIC reserves grow to reflect the true and clear dangers to the industry, the taxpayers of America are at risk.

This taxpayer risk has a direct effect on you, the consumer. First of all, the consumer pays for the FDIC insurance. Banks are charged a fee for the coverage, which they pass on to the customer in the form of higher direct costs. So don't think you are getting something for nothing. You're not.

Here is a more pressing consumer problem. Many people, especially the elderly, will invest only with an institution that offers FDIC insurance. They strongly consider the supposed security factor. That means that banks have a government-assisted edge in the supposedly free market. Yet, that insurance may be more of a myth than reality. As the FSLIC collapse and subsequent S&L bailout prove conclusively, when you rely on government-backed deposit insurance you are, in effect, insuring your money yourself. Why should you care? Because banks historically offer investment and savings rates below their real market value, which means bank customers are losing *additional* revenue possibilities due to their desire for very questionable FDIC insurance.

The truth is, most major companies have better "insurance" through their corporate financial structure than do banks through the FDIC. The bottom line? The security-seeking customer is being sold a bill of goods by the banks and the government, a very costly bill of goods that may soon become even more expensive.

For those that may think my opinion alarmist, I refer you to Japan's banking industry. Just a few short years ago, that's the model America's bankers urged us to follow. Like Japan, they aimed for less regulation, access to more markets and to more international markets, more government assistance, more risky real estate investments. Look at Japan's banking industry today. It's in shambles, and may collapse completely. Yet this is the model we are, in large part, still pursuing.

Government Protects Unscrupulous Bankers

When a shareholder or depositor having a problem with a national bank writes the federal agency charged with supervising the national banking system, he or she invariably receives the following response: "We, as a matter of policy, do not disclose information that may or may not have been obtained in the course of an investigation." With this simple, but all-inclusive statement, the comptroller of the currency, administrator of national banks, dismisses virtually all inquiries concerning a national bank. Generally, the FDIC and state banking authorities are likewise unresponsive. This secrecy catchall represents a major cause of the high number of bank closings.

Shareholders who, by their votes, could remove and replace

directors, and therefore bank management, are forbidden access to the substantive information that would allow them an educated appraisal of those technically in their employ. Worse yet, if a shareholder or depositor knows of any wrongdoing within a bank, he cannot receive confirmation of the offense or an outline of any corrective or punitive actions taken. Since the majority of bank directors and officers guilty of a malfeasance are given the opportunity to resign, as opposed to being prosecuted (to spare embarrassment to the bank), even the most outrageous banker abuses go unpunished. And it's all done in secret.

A depositor with a problem has the same difficulty as unsatisfied or concerned shareholders. The government will not voluntarily make available information that may help the depositor with a case, even if the bank or banker has been convicted of illegalities. Regulatory agencies are so dedicated to protecting banks from public scrutiny that they not only don't make available the results of their investigations, they also won't even acknowledge whether an investigation has taken place.

Government agencies also hide behind the same secrecy that protects the banks. This allows the comptroller the luxury of presenting publicly only those facts that are flattering to himself and his office. No one can receive any information about their national bank if the Comptroller, at his office's sole discretion, decides not to be of assistance. Based on my experience, this is the option employed almost 100 percent of the time. As you can imagine, the office takes every opportunity to use secrecy to the benefit of the suspect bank. The comptroller is even exempt from legitimate Congressional review. The comptroller's office, like all agencies that supervise financial institutions, operates outside public scrutiny. It is even protected from Freedom of Information Act requests.

Bankers say they need federal protection from public review and accountability to prevent a possible repeat of the Depression-era run on banks—while, when soliciting our deposits, reassuring that panic can never reoccur. As bankers often do, they offer history when it suits their purposes, and ask us to forget it when it doesn't. By their actions, bankers and the government demonstrate that they don't believe we are educated enough to cope with the truth. The S&L crisis and the record number of bank closings would indicate their rationale for secrecy is not working.

Unfortunately, consumers and shareholders of banks are not receiving assistance from their elected representatives in Congress with this crucial issue. The following quote from former Senator Jake Garn, then chairman of the Committee on Banking, Housing and Urban Affairs, demonstrates the magnitude of resistance by our legislators to full banking disclosure: "I also believe that the examination and supervisory activities conducted by the federal bank regulatory agencies are most efficiently conducted without public disclosure at every step of the process." He, and the majority of elected officials that subscribe to his position, couldn't be more wrong.

Banks, when presented with a business loan request, will turn a corporation inside out for information, ordering audits, requiring personal guarantees, demanding personal financial statements from corporate staff, along with many other requirements, before they will make a lending decision. Yet, they fight viciously (through the ABA) to ensure their own freedom from the obligation to offer their shareholders and depositors all but the very minimum of cursory financial information about the bank. How can a shareholder know if management needs to be replaced? How can a depositor know whether or not he or she should do business with a specific bank? The answer is obvious: They can't.

But the damaging effect of regulatory secrecy can become even more costly. A case in point: During congressional hearings on the Penn Square bank closing, then Comptroller of the Currency C. T. Conover admitted that his staff had known of the bank's critical condition as many as two years in advance of its closing. His office made private recommendations to the bank and then gave the bank's staff time to take appropriate corrective actions. It would be logical to assume that giving the same people that caused the problems time to correct them might do more harm than good. It did. The bank's deficiency nearly tripled during that period. The same type of progression occurred with the savings-and-loan bailout—if the government had acted immediately, the cost would have been approximately five billion dollars—instead of forty to one hundred times that. History strongly suggests that time never helps in these situations. In the case of Penn Square, time worked against the shareholders, depositors, and later, other banks. Banks that had large participation loans (loans made to a single borrower funded by a group of banks) with Penn Square, such as Continental Illinois National Bank, suffered huge second-level loan losses. If the government had gone public with Penn Square's problems immediately, much of the long-term damage would never have happened.

Shareholders of a bank deserve a complete accounting of the bank's condition at all times. They should be warned when the government discovers bank improprieties. After all, it is their investment money that will be lost if the bank is closed (shareholders' monies are *not* protected by the FDIC). It is their money that will be lost due to profit runoff caused by inept, unprofessional management. It is their money that will be lost due to embezzlement. Yet, the very people that hold 100 percent financial liability for uninsured bank losses are prohibited from learning anything of substance that would protect their investment!

And if this secrecy doctrine ever leads to a national banking collapse; the taxpayer will be handed the bill. All of us have monetary exposure to the decisions made by banks and government regulatory agencies. Yet, they do not grant protection of our assets priority. The government believes it is in its best interest to keep marginal banks open as long as possible, as each closing is a threat to the larger system and the bureaucracy of regulatory agencies. To the end of self-preservation, the comptroller and others have chosen to *perpetuate* instead of *regulate*. Each time a bank is given additional time to correct its deficiencies when it should be closed, the government is betting the monies of innocent investors and taxpayers. The truth is, if a bank's affairs are in such disarray that public knowledge of the facts would cause a run on the bank, the bank should be closed—immediately! In this manner, shareholder, depositor, and taxpayer losses would be minimized. If the bank is to remain open in the hope of correcting what appears to be inevitable, it should be done only with the informed approval of everyone with a financial interest.

Bank shareholders and depositors should be informed of serious or potentially serious matters concerning their bank. To name a few: Are bank officers being paid excessive compensation? Are directors or officers guilty of illegal insider transactions or bank stock trading? Has the bank experienced any embezzlements? Is bank management qualified and performing up to industry standards? Are bank loan losses in excess of the norm for this bank's peer group? Is the bank on the FDIC's problem list? Is the bank under any cease-and-desist order(s) (a legal order to stop a certain activity)? Is the bank about to be closed? The government will not offer this information even upon direct inquiry. It has failed to realize that secrecy protects no one but the guilty or unprofessional banker.

Bankers are members of the most exclusive and secret club in America. Sadly, the public is denied access, even though we're the ones who pay their dues.

Banking's Drug Connection

Drug trafficking is a "business" that, by the nature of its currency volume, makes major dealers immediately recognizable to authorities if they cannot discreetly launder their ill-gotten gains. Some banks have become the willing answer to the dealer's problem.

It's common knowledge in the banking community that certain banks have catered to the lucrative money-laundering trade. A prima facie case is made every time a bank opens and, in mere months, boasts assets in excess of what a normal bank would take decades to acquire, or an existing bank suddenly experiences extraordinary asset growth attributable to but a few seemingly nondescript accounts. The connection is reliably established each time a bank fails to fulfill or pleads guilty to violating the federal requirement of reporting large currency transactions. Although fines have been levied, this is not typically a transgression that sends bankers to jail. One major bank, after admitting currency violations, stated that even after paying its six-figure fine, it still made a substantial profit. This story, like the example of the high-flying S&L operators who got away with billions, proves that—contrary to the adage—if you're a "respectable" bank or banker willing to step over the line, crime does pay.

Since that fine was levied, other banks have come forward to admit reporting violations. However, because of back-room deals with the government, they have not usually been required to confess wrongdoing. At best, some banks have admitted to making honest mistakes. Nevertheless, it strains credulity to believe that financial institutions would willingly pay a large fine without a fight if they had not knowingly participated in the illegal acts for which they are being disciplined. Banks are not wont to give money away.

The bankers' "honest mistake" defense puts even more strain on their already questionable credibility. From where do they think an inordinate amount of money, brought in day after day after day, might come? Are bankers really so naive or incompetent? Of course not. Those far less affluent than bankers have been sent to jail for complicity on far less evidence. Unfortunately, banks and bankers have become virtually immune to prosecution even though a case can be fairly made that some are every bit as guilty as the suppliers and pushers of sponsoring the unabated drug trade. They're not there at the start of the transaction, nor during, but they're there at the end when the profits are counted. They are using the respectibility of their industry and institutions to profit without regard for their crucial part in the crime.

Every once in awhile the banking-drug connection is so blatant that a banker takes a fall, but in most cases the bank itself gets a pass. Such was the recent case of a senior officer for a large money-center bank who was convicted of laundering thirty million for a drug cartel headquartered in Mexico. At the time of the trial, the officer was working in the bank's Miami office. A spokesman for the bank in New York was reported as saying that the bank was disappointed by the verdict. More than likely, what disappointed the bank was was that the officer got caught. How could others in the bank be unaware of what was happening? How much in the way of fees did the bank make on the deal? It doesn't matter; the bank itself was exonerated.

Another aspect of the bank-drug connection that demands scrutiny is the relationship between participating banks and drug-producing nations. These countries, many of which owe U.S. banks billions of dollars, are protected from retribution for their drug activities because the federal government fears that positive actions to stop drugs at their source would necessarily precipitate an economic drain on the guilty countries, and that could force them to default on their U.S. bank loans. This vested-interest logic, presented to Congress and the President by bankers; says, any tangible actions will cause a catastrophic ripple effect on the U.S. banking system. That lie or threat has always culminated in congressional complicity. Of course, banks charging off foreign debt, however large and for whatever reason, simply means the free market is at work, but not so in the case of this cycle of deceit.

Money-laundering can and should be stopped immediately. Fines greatly eclipsing a bank's profit on money-laundering must be levied, and participating bankers need personally to feel the full force of the law. Banks should be forced immediately to start charging off delinquent debt from drug exporting nations. If accomplished over an extended period of time, this strategy would allow affected banks to stay in business without taxpayer assistance, while at the same time strengthening their balance sheets by eliminating nonperforming loans that are being falsely represented as assets. More important, it would remove the protective umbrella from drug cartels and nations that are slowly killing our addicted citizens, many of whom are children.

Why have I included this subject? Because no other topic reveals the power of the banking industry and its thirst for profits at any cost better than its drug connection. It also exposes the lie that the government is supervising the industry for the betterment of consumers-citizens. The truth is, government only cares that a bank is profitable. How it becomes profitable is not of concern.

A Catastrophe in the Making

The General Accounting Office has estimated the S&L collapse bailout will ultimately cost taxpayers (principal plus interest) up to five hundred billion dollars. Independent assessments range up to a trillion dollars. Regardless of the actual cost, we've experienced the largest financial debacle in history, a disaster that could not have occurred if regulators and Congress had done their jobs.

Surely a lesson had been learned; surely the same fate would not visit the more crucial banking industry. Everyone assumed that regulators would increase bank supervision to ameliorate their previously inadequate efforts and Congress would take its attendant oversight responsibility more seriously to ensure no further damage to taxpayers. However, I have discovered that regulators still routinely allow banks to violate laws and banking regulations and that Congress—specifically the House Banking, House and Urban Affairs Committee and the Senate Banking, Finance and Urban Affairs Committee—is doing everything in its power to ensure that the public never knows the extent of the incestuous relationship between banks and those charged with their oversight.

The hows and whys of the S&L collapse are simple. While contributing factors, the Federal Home Loan Bank Board (FHLBB), the Federal Savings and Loan Insurance Corporation (FSLIC), and Congress weren't taken by surprise by the combined effects of deregulation, the acts of unscrupulous bankers, and the state of the economy. The tragedy was the result of an inability of regulators and Congress to prioritize correctly their obligation to protect taxpayers above all else. Bank regulators are now following the same dire path, and Congress is continuing its malpractice and calling it "reform." Both remain, mistakenly, in the business of protecting banks—a failed policy that has already cost billions.

To be of assistance in the "reform" debate, I contacted the House and Senate banking committees in May of 1991, requesting the privilege of presenting documented evidence of banking and regulatory abuses. Unfortunately, after more than a year's worth of work, stacks of letters, and almost daily phone calls, both committees refused even to look at my presentation.

The representatives expressed two revealing sentiments to explain the stonewalling. One House member said he wouldn't personally review the documents, nor recommend that his subcommittee do so, because what I was implying couldn't possibly be true. He went on to state that regulators were thoroughly professional and did an exemplary job. A Senate committee counsel divulged something even more alarming than the uninformed congressman. He stated the reason his committee wouldn't look at my presentation or allow testimony was that members knew what I was saying was true, but it would be harmful to bring the malfeasance to the public's view, as they couldn't possibly understand the problem and the inferences they might draw would be dangerous. Insultingly, Congress is quick to oblige innocent taxpayers to pay for the mistakes of bankers, yet don't feel we are intelligent enough to deal with the details that occasioned the debt.

The banking industry, as we are so often told by the American Banker's Association, is highly regulated. That's true. The problem is that the comptroller of the currency, administrator of national banks; the FDIC; and the Federal Reserve Board of Governors won't enforce compliance. For example, the industry has recently been subject to a host of public-disclosure laws, such as the Community Reinvestment Act. Notwithstanding the altruistic intentions of such laws, if a bank doesn't comply with a disclosure request, the applicable regulatory agency will do nothing to require it and assess fines—the law, therefore, becomes meaningless.

Freedom of Information Act requests are too frequently denied, and even those that are honored often take months, rather than the mandated ten working days from time of receipt, to be answered. Shareholders or consumers having a problem with their bank are likewise denied assistance by regulators. Typically, petitioners are told the agency does not become involved in "private disputes," even if the dispute involves a violation of law by a bank or banker. Again, protection of the institution is the uppermost consideration.

I discovered other abuses, among them apparent illegal ownership of land, violation of the Depository Management Interlocks Act, false statements to shareholders, failure to file proper change-of-ownership notices, inaccurate and incomplete merger/stock prospectuses, failure to file oath-of-director forms, insider trading, and published call reports that don't balance. These violations, while legally significant, more importantly represent a trespass of principle. When banking regulators don't enforce the laws, they encourage bankers to ignore banking ethics whenever it is profitable, and that practice paves the path to another taxpayer bailout. It was no coincidences that The S&L collapse it was precipitated by the supervisory ethical collapse of the FHLBB and the FSLIC. This historical reference is important because the same laissez-faire attitude of S&L regulators yesterday is being practiced by bank regulators today.

And Congress still isn't meeting its obligation of guardianship. Perhaps that's because, as bankers are always boasting at their Miami or Hawaiian conventions, "We have the best Congress money can buy."

Now that you know how the banking industry is ripping off the public at large, let's look at how your own bank is ripping you off personally.

LOANS

The ABCs of Bank Credit

Financial success is predicated on either having money or being able to obtain it. Many times, being able to borrow money paves the way eventually to keeping it. For this reason, understanding how your bank arrives at an answer to your loan requests is the first step to successful, intelligent, profitable borrowing.

The basis for any loan decision should be an assessment of the Five Cs of Credit: character, capacity, capital, collateral, and conditions. Your bank obtains this information in a variety of ways—directly from you in the application and loan-interview process, and through a credit check. Before exploring specifically how the bank gathers this information, let's review the banker's Five Cs, what they are, how they are applied, and how they should be applied.

Character: This should be, and historically has been, the most important of the Five Cs. An applicant with unquestionable character often was approved for a loan that otherwise might be rejected. Character, from the banker's point of view, is most often obtained from a credit report. In a small town it may be determined by reputation or family ties.

The critical criterion is your payment record, specifically your payment record with the bank to which you're applying. Although in general you want to shop loan requests and have accounts at many institutions, an established payment record is one reason to use the same financial institutions again and again. Of course, I am assuming you are comfortable with a particular bank's rates and services.

Capacity: In this context capacity is simply a measure of your ability to repay the debt. Successful people with substantial salaries receive a high score. Others do not.

Capital: This is the amount of money/assets you have at your disposal. It measures financial acumen, your ability to use your salary/finances wisely.

Collateral: Collateral is the bank's insurance policy on your loan. It is anything you own and pledge to the bank—land, home, business, car, etc.—that could be sold to raise cash to pay off your loan. It can't make a bad loan good, but it can make a good loan better. Collateral alone, without cash flow to pay the monthly expense, will not be enough to ensure loan approval. However, a slight deficiency in one area of the request might be offset by additional collateral if it's available.

Conditions: Condition considerations are usually reserved for business loan requests. For example, during a recession it would probably not be prudent for a bank to be loaning money for marginal new business ventures. The economic conditions of the moment would obviously have a negative impact on the loan request regardless of the loan's actual merit.

For the individual customer, even though economic conditions don't usually affect the consumer per se, they may affect the loan officer's state of mind, which is then factored into the decision.

That's the way I learned the Five Cs some twenty-five years ago. Today, unfortunately, the Five Cs of Credit have been reduced to the Three Cs of Credit: Capital, collateral, and conditions.

Banker's greed is the reason for the diminished Five Cs of Credit. There was a time when a community bank's loan-making priority was to the individual borrower. Those days are gone. The big borrower is what the banks are looking for, because it requires less bank staff servicing expense, and that means more net profit. For example, a million-dollar commercial credit is equal to one hundred auto loans at ten thousand dollars each. A billion-dollar credit is worth twenty thousand mortgage loans at fifty thousand dollars each.

With this profit mania in mind, let's review the Three Cs of Credit as they are probably practiced at your local bank.

Capital: Capital, to the modern banker's thinking, means that if you have one thousand dollars deposited in the banker's bank as collateral, he is more than willing to loan you five hundred dollars. It's an extension of the banker's credo: "If you don't need the money, we are eager to lend it to you."

What the banks really want is to loan huge sums of money to large corporations that are financially liquid, stable, and profitable. In their eyes, that is the safest loan possible. But theirs is a misplaced value judgment.

Banks as an industry have failed to see that their truly dependable market is the individual depositor. Without them, the bank would close. Consequently, individuals' lending needs should be met. Granted, it's easier to service a large commercial loan, but all those fancy corporate financial statements offered as loan collateral aren't necessarily worth the paper they're written on. If that weren't the case, why the record number of corporate bankruptcies? Think of what one major charge-off for a bad corporate loan does to the bank's financial statement.

Because of the bank's attitude toward risk, you must convey the image of not really needing to borrow the money you're requesting. You have to convey affluence, and that means you must—legitimately, and legally—inflate your personal financial statement (see page 63). Convincing the loan officer that you actually don't *need* the loan is absolutely mandatory for quick loan approval and subsequent loan-rate negotiations.

Collateral: Collateral should have no bearing on the loan officer's decision. The loan should stand or fall on its own merits. However, bankers like to feel secure, so they'll demand more and more collateral until they think they have a risk-free loan. Use caution before you offer your dearest possessions for this purpose.

Good loan officers know that cash flow and personal character are far more important than collateral. Repossessed collateral can be worthless. It can be "lost" or destroyed. It can be worth ten cents on the dollar. Despite these facts, most loan officers will demand excessive collateralization.

Obtaining a home mortgage is a good example of the industry's excessive collateral requirements. Typically, the bank wants a 20 percent to 30 percent down payment. On a $100,000.00 home, that down payment assures that the bank, through the mortgage agreement, has a twenty-to thirty-thousand-dollar equity cushion in case of your default. Additionally, homes generally appreciate in value. Therefore, the bank's equity position improves each and every year, as the mortgage balance goes down while the property's value goes up. In short, a mortgage is a bank's safest loan. Yet home mortgage rates continue to far exceed the bank's actual exposure to risk.

The banker's demand for excessive collateral is another reason you must continually convince the bank that you are not just another customer. Image cultivation will grant you special considerations others will not receive.

Once you do accomplish a profitable banking relationship, you can then use your collateral to obtain interest-rate reductions. Most customers offer collateral as an inducement for loan approval. Educated customers have created a financial persona that by itself will receive a positive response; at that point they offer collateral in exchange for a lower interest rate. (We'll discuss how to do this later in the book.)

If you don't learn how to play your collateral card, your collateral will at best help you get the loan, nothing more.

Conditions: In tough times, good banks excel and make more money than ever, while the marginal, poorly managed banks flounder. This interesting paradox gives the wise consumer excellent borrowing opportunities. If you have established yourself in the marketplace, you will always have access to money. Your cost of money may escalate, but you'll be able to get it, and that's the important thing. This is critical, as some of the best investment opportunities are available during those times when the average consumer couldn't borrow a dime if his or her life depended on it. If you've convinced the bank that they need you more than you need them, you will be able to avail yourself of this profitable fact of financial life: There is always money to be borrowed—the only question is, who gets to borrow it? You want to spend time and effort ensuring that the answer to that question is *you*.

One of the great lessons of the Depression is that while many fortunes were lost, many fortunes were made. Those that had access to money were in the driver's seat. They bought valuable assets for pennies on the dollar.

This has been true throughout history, yet most people ignore it. The economy is cyclical. Those prepared for the pendulum swing will reap its benefits. That's why you have to cultivate your lending relationship with a number of banks—and nonbanks— and be ready to take advantage of economic conditions.

The final step in the credit decision is the credit check.

In order to ensure borrowing success, I strongly recommend that you write for or take a trip to the local credit bureau to see your file before your banker does.

You have a legal right to see your credit file at any time.

The bureau does have the authority to charge a fair fee for that service (usually under twenty dollars), so don't be surprised if there is a nominal fee.

Most credit bureaus are unreliable due to the crushing volume of data they process. Mistakes are made daily. Erroneous data may be on your history that could cost you your loan. The most common problem is that bureaus rarely remove disputed credit information from a file. These disagreements can show up as nonpayments and ruin your rating.

Obviously, you want to make sure the bureau doesn't report errors to your bank regarding your credit history. More important, if there is some bad news on the report, even unfavorable correct information, you can lessen its impact at the bank. For example, if there is a late payment, you can explain to the loan officer that you had a problem that will probably show up on your credit report, but it was a disputed charge you legitimately refused to pay. The point of this "head 'em off at the pass" approach is that the banker will be impressed with your honesty. He or she will never know that you told out of necessity. In short, you have taken a real negative and turned it into a positive.

If the credit bureau has made a mistake on your account, let them know that you expect it to be cleared immediately. They will comply, because if you're denied credit due to their error, you can file suit to collect damages. They know that, so they are willing to respond to an aggressive consumer.

Unfortunately, bankers rely only on three criteria in making credit decisions: capital, collateral, and conditions. Now you know. Understanding the credit decision and how it works is the key to making the lending system work for you instead of against you.

How to Protect Yourself When You Borrow from the Bank

There was a time not long ago when you could borrow money from a bank and didn't have to worry, because you were going to be treated fairly. Those days are gone. Your banker is not your friend. As I've already said, he or she is more likely an enemy. I don't care what the advertisements say. I don't care if the loan officer was your Sunday school teacher. The fact is, bankers are friendly only when it suits their purposes. But if things get a little ragged around the edges and you're a few days late with your loan payment, they'll rip out your heart to protect the bank. Actually, it's more to protect themselves and their cushy jobs. Loan officers don't stay employed, much less get ahead, by making loans that are delinquent and/or have to be charged off. As they say in the boxing ring, you must protect yourself at all times. If you don't protect your interests, who will? The following five rules will help:

1. Get it in writing. No matter what the circumstances, get all promises in writing. Otherwise your banker may have a convenient lapse in memory at a very inconvenient time. For example, many people can attest that they had a verbal mortgage loan commitment at X percent, only to find out later that their deal was no longer valid because "rates changed" and so had loan fees. Of course, this usually only happens when rates go up.

Don't depend, no matter what type of loan you're looking for, on what the banker says regarding terms and rates—get it in writing. It is almost impossible to protect yourself legally if you don't. The courts normally side with the bank if you decide to sue regarding a loan matter that was not committed to paper. It's just your word against theirs, and judges have a hard time believing that a bank would lie.

2. Understand what you're signing. Of course, the bank doesn't care if you understand your loan documents (as explained earlier). In fact, they would probably prefer that you didn't; that way, if there are problems, they will have the upper hand. Loan documents are one-sided to start with. If you don't read and understand everything in them, you're in big trouble. Ask questions if you're confused. If need be, and especially if the loan is substantial, have an attorney review the document. It will cost a few bucks, probably less than $100, but it may be worth it, especially for small-business loans. It's mandatory for a mortgage.

3. If you can't afford to lose it, don't pledge it. This is an especially appropriate admonishment since the Tax Reform Act of 1986; which spawned home-equity credit lines. Since the interest on standard borrowing is no longer tax-deductible, many banks repackaged their second-mortgage loans into home-equity credit lines, meaning you pledge your house as collateral against a loan. They're not a good deal. The fees are excessive, and, in many cases, you end up spending two dollars in costs and extra interest in order to save one dollar in taxes. But that's not the biggest problem. When you pledge your home—even for a small loan of a few thousand dollars—and you're delinquent, the bank will go after your home to protect itself. Think about that: You could lose your home for a vacation loan or some other insignificant borrowing. All because your bank wanted to make a few extra bucks at your expense by appealing to your sense of greed via its sales pitch; Borrow this way, because it will save taxes! Again, while a home-equity loan might save taxes, the loan may still be a net loser; but more important, it may be the riskiest loan you ever sign.

4. Never waive your rights. Banks make mistakes—every day. The public would be stunned if they knew how many errors, big ones, the banks commit. The reason that's not common knowledge is that banks are good at covering their tracks, and there is no legitimate government oversight.

One of the best tricks banks use when they realize they've made a mistake that might cause a civil lawsuit is to call the abused customers and tell them they need to change some aspect of their loan. They might even offer better terms, a bigger credit line, or something else as an incentive. But, along with the good news they usually include a waiver of some sort. Quite often it is hidden from general view and is couched in bankerese. Thus you must carefully review all your documentation when dealing with your bank and don't waive any of your rights, ever.

5. If you have a problem, act immediately. The statute of limitations regarding banking matters may come into play if you wait too long to take action. More likely, you will have problems if you don't act immediately because of the "waiver of fraud." Simply put, after discovering that your bank has defrauded you, if you continue the transaction in anyway, you may have waived your rights to sue.

If you're not sure of your rights, call the agencies listed in the Appendix (see page 172) or consult an attorney.

While it makes no sense to consider suing the bank for every small indiscretion, it does pay to raise the issue with a bank officer immediately so as to protect your rights. Remember, in America, the party with the most money—and therefore the best legal representation—usually wins a dispute. The bottom line is, your bank has more money than you. Your bank has the help and assistance of the state and federal government. Under the best of circumstances you are at a disadvantage in a bank dispute. If you wait to take action, your position is almost always lost.

Remember, no matter what type of loan we're talking about,

if you don't protect your interests, no one will. Don't trust the bank. Don't trust the loan officer. Don't trust the fine print in the bank's boilerplate loan contract.

In the last few years bankers have been very active in pushing government to change consumer-protection laws to better protect the banks. In most cases they've been successful. It is becoming more and more difficult for a customer to win a legal battle with a bank, even if he or she is in the right. It is becoming easier and easier for a bank to sue a customer and win, even if the bank is in the wrong. I hope that paradox will get your attention and cause you to take action to protect yourself before you have a problem too.

Should I Borrow Money or Not?

Borrowing money can be an expensive proposition, especially if you borrow when you don't need to.

Quite simply, you should never borrow to purchase depreciating assets (assets that decrease in value with the passage of time). You should borrow for things that you *have* to have, necessities such as housing. Borrow for your business. Borrow to make money (investments). Borrow when the cost of borrowing is less than the predictable inflationary increase of the purchase (example: when inflation was at 15 percent and mortgages were at 9 percent), providing a built-in profitmaker. These are reasons to borrow. You shouldn't borrow for vacations, TV sets, and other luxury items. Why? Because you're never going to get ahead or stay even when you are paying more for things than they're actually worth (that is, at a cost over and above retail or resale value). This small tip can save you thousands of dollars throughout your financial lifetime. Has your banker ever told you this sobering fact? Probably not. More likely he was more than willing to finance depreciating asset purchases at a high-interest installment loan rate.

Of course, it's important to know where best to borrow money once you've determined that a loan is necessary. Generally speaking, you should never finance a purchase through the seller of a product. Most of us will be tempted to do so when we buy a car. The dealer will tell you that he will arrange financing, do the paperwork, process the application, and so on, and you won't have to do any legwork or be inconvenienced. Many salesmen will tell you that this is the best financing available because it comes directly from the bank.

What the salesman won't tell you is that, although the bank will finance the loan, the car dealer will get a kickback from the bank at your expense. How does this work? Very simply, if your rate should have been 7 percent, you will be quoted a rate of one to three percentage points higher, because you're dealing through a middleman. The difference goes to the dealer without your knowledge. A $10,000.00 car loan for forty-eight months could cost you another $1,200.00 over and above what the bank would have quoted you had you gone to the bank on your own. Has your banker ever told you that they cut under-the-table deals like this at their customers' expense? I doubt it.

Finance companies get their money from banks or investors, and then reloan it to the consumer. That's why it's so expensive to borrow from finance companies. They pass on their cost of borrowing and add to it their profit margin. There is also an added greed factor, because they know people that borrow from them don't understand the system or have no other way to borrow money. Obviously, you should never borrow from a finance company.

No matter who or what is involved, you should never allow anyone to arrange your financing. You can't afford it.

Despite their disadvantages, banks are a constant source of credit, and one you should consider as an option. The problem is that banks offer a very unfair form of lending for most consumer loans. It's called an installment loan. We'll get to that later.

Of course, no matter what your loan needs, you should explore all your options. These are explained in detail in the Appendix under "Banking Alternatives" (see page 176). But before you borrow from any source, you have to ensure that there isn't a better way to obtain the money you need. As best as you can, heed the admonishment, "Neither a borrower nor a lender be."

How to Determine How Much You Can Afford to Borrow Safely

There is no greater credit pitfall then allowing yourself to become overextended. Your bank, however, wants you borrowed to the hilt and beyond, especially if you are using an installment loan or credit card as your lending vehicle. The bank's return on personal loans is so huge due to interest charges that the consumer's financial well-being is trampled by the banker's lust for maximum profits. Your banker, if he is to meet the service intent of his bank's charter, should be offering loans that are prudent for both the bank and the customer. Unfortunately, many bankers ignore their guidance responsibility and focus only on the positive impact your loan will have on the bank's bottom line.

Banks, when dealing in loans that have lower returns (mortgages, for example), are very conservative in their lending decisions. With loans that have enormous returns (credit cards, for instance) they are truly liberal. This ludicrous disparity is directly proportionate to the bank's profit margin on each loan type. If you're buying a highly secured home mortgage at 9 percent, they run you through the wringer and want every *i* dotted and *t* crossed. If you're using a credit card at 19 percent they couldn't care less what you buy, when you buy it, and/or if you can afford it.

The bank's misplaced regard for your credit-paying abilities shouldn't cloud your borrowing decisions. You yourself must know, based on your ability to repay, what your borrowing parameters are. Don't base that answer on limits set by the bank. Their vested interest(s) are a reflection of their profit expectations. You need an answer based on your own desires tempered by your financial realities.

Although I am against borrowing for most of the usual purposes, let's assume here that you have a legitimate reason for purchasing money. There is a method of ascertaining if your borrowing is in line with your income. This rule of thumb should be applied without rationalization to be effective. You may be shocked to find out you're woefully overextended.

Take your after-tax income, subtract your housing and auto expense, and multiply the answer by 12 percent (.12). It's that simple. The answer indicates the total outstanding additional debt you can reasonably afford. The proportion of most family budgets devoted to debt will exceed this test, as we as a nation have been conditioned (in large part by the banking industry) to hold excessive credit obligations. But that doesn't mean it's right. If you're overextended, it's time for some changes, no matter how inconvenient.

Let's look at an example. A family with an after-tax income of $30,000.00, a housing expense of $750 per month (take into account the rent or mortgage, taxes, maintenance, and insurance) or $9,000.00 per year, and a car expense of $250 per month, or $3,000 per year, should have an additional debt not to exceed $2,160. ($30,000 − 9,000 − 3,000 = 18,000 × .12 = 2,160). That debt ceiling should include all your other obligations, regardless of how or why they originated.

Surprised? Think the total is too small? It's not. If you're above your limit you shouldn't panic. However, do use this exercise as a blueprint for change.

How serious is the principle of understanding the relationship of debt to your ability to repay? It is critical! A case in point is made every time another former millionaire files bankruptcy. The millionaire had income, he had assets—what he didn't have was control of his debt.

And your bank's role in all this? It is one of the major purveyors of easy, overpriced credit. As long as its return is enormous it will ignore the basic lending principles of the Five Cs of Credit. It will also ignore its responsibility to provide guidance to its customers. When we consult other professionals, we expect to receive advice that is appropriate for our circumstances; that is, the best service at the lowest possible cost. But the bank does just the opposite. It offers the worst possible solution—high-priced credit—for the very people who, for their own good, should be denied. Far too many banks will be more than happy to extend you expensive credit in excess of what is safe for your financial situation. While interest rates should be a reflection of exposure to risk, your credit limit shouldn't be set by the same criterion.

Bankers know that, yet they are willing to ignore what is best for you if their profit is large enough.

Protect yourself. No matter what you pay for money, you shouldn't exceed what you can afford. Don't let any lender ruin your future by offering you high-priced "easy" money. And even when you get a good deal on credit, don't borrow more than you can afford.

Loan Rates Are Negotiable

One thing most borrowers fail to understand is that loan rates are negotiable. Every year consumers pay millions more in interest than they should because they are unaware of this fact.

Unfortunately, in most lending transactions the borrower is at a distinct disadvantage. To some degree this is due to the imbalance in the lender-borrower relationship. After all, getting a loan is often more important to the individual than the cost of losing that individual's business is to the bank. The fact that all aspects of the transaction will take place on the banker's turf further inhibits the customer. A great many features of the loan process are planned by the bank to intimidate customers. Making you wait to see the loan officer is part of the plan. Having confusing loan forms is part of the plan. Offering only one loan vehicle, usually an installment loan, is part of the plan. The bank knows if you're intimidated you won't even consider asking for a loan-rate reduction. You'll be so happy just to receive loan approval that you wouldn't dare ask to negotiate your interest rate.

The aim of most loan officers is to make you feel less than worthy. In effect, regardless of how long you have been a valued bank customer, you'll have to convince the loan officer that you are trustworthy. Never mind your standing in the community. Never mind your work record. Never mind your exemplary credit rating. With planned intimidation, banks help preserve their unfair schedule of loan rates.

Most banks have one rate per type of loan. They charge X percent for prime, X plus percent for home mortgages, X plus.

plus percent for car loans, and so on. The reason for lumping loan rates by catagory as opposed to the individual's creditworthiness is that the bank wants to let the good customers pay for the mistakes they make with the bad customers.

Let's review the situations of two bank-loan customers who are buying the same type of car, with the same price tag. One has been a bank customer for ten years, has paid 60 percent down on the car, and needs the loan for only twenty-four months. In addition, he has a perfect credit rating at the bank and elsewhere. The other customer has been with the bank six months, has paid 5 percent down, needs the loan for forty-eight months, and has a marginal credit rating. What rate will both these customers be quoted? Regardless of the rate, it will be the same in each case. Again, the bank is going to charge the good customer more than he deserves in case the marginal customer defaults. That's the way banks do business.

According to the "free market" theory that bankers always claim they're following, that policy is in direct contradiction to the fact that loan interest rates are supposed to be a direct reflection of the bank's exposure to risk on each request. Therefore, if we are to take the bankers at their word, these customers should have differing interest rates—substantially different rates.

A good bank, one staffed by fair and knowledgeable loan officers, will balance its loan portfolio on a risk basis. Bad banks, those unresponsive to the needs of their communities, lump their rates by category. You have to avoid the latter at all costs. You cannot afford to pay the bank more interest on each and every loan so they can absorb loan losses from others.

How can you combat this frontal assault? Obviously you have to shop for banking services. A loan request should be shopped at a minimum of three financial institutions. Ideally, you'll explore other, nontraditional avenues as well, as mentioned throughout the book.

Over and above that, you should remember this valuable rule of thumb. Bank at the smallest, or one of the smaller, financial institutions in your market area. The smaller bank needs you; the big bank doesn't. With the smaller bank you have some leverage, at the big bank, you don't. For instance, a $9,000 car loan at a $20 million bank is the equivalent of a $9 million loan at a $20 billion bank. That added leverage will help your loan-rate negotiations. Most big banks have an arrogant attitude, which is going to cost you money in the form of added loan interest. Regardless of the bank you choose, you should always negotiate your loan rate. (This works for interest rates on savings as well—they're negotiable too.)

You have to convince your bank, without being abusive, that you are financially savvy. You know how the system works, and you are not willing to pay extra for the bank's delinquent loan problems. Further, you see yourself as the bank's best possible loan risk, meaning that, based on your credit history and banking relationship, you aren't a risk at all. And, just like General Motors, you expect to be in the bank's lowest loan-rate category.

Use whatever dialogue fits your style. You'll find this positioning isn't as hard as it may at first sound. Actually, it's quite easy once you get the hang of it.

Here are a few suggestions that will help.

1. Ask for a better rate—sometimes that's all it takes, the gumption to ask.

2. Call around to a number of outlets so you know what the market will bear and then play one bank against the other by saying, "Can you beat the rate they're offering down the street?"

3. Have all your facts and figures in hand instead of appearing financially uneducated when asked questions.

4. Have a fall-back position, such as moving your accounts if you're dealing with a new bank, if you can get a better loan rate, or be prepared to pick up your chips and go home if your present bank isn't willing to give you a fair deal.

5. Understand that the profit margin on bank loans is so large that there is room for the bank to lower your rate and still make a substantial profit—so if your banker tells you there's nothing he can do except offer the rate they're offering everyone, politely ask to see this person's supervisor and plead your case. Bankers don't like people going over their head.

6. In most cases you'll have to do nothing more than suggestion 1—ask for a better deal.

I appear on radio call-in shows throughout the country on a fairly regular basis. Whenever I recommend this strategy to callers they almost invariably say that they can't bargain with their bank. To that I answer that their bank's intentional intimidation of its customer base has worked. Don't fall for it, especially if you've been a customer for a long time, are willing to move accounts to their bank, and you have a good credit rating.

More often than not when I return to that station those same people will call back and say that I was right, that all they had to do was ask and they got a better deal. One elderly gentleman I remember called back months later and was furious—not with me, but with the fact that he didn't have this information sooner. He said he now knows, because he got a lower interest rate on his car loan simply by asking, that he could have saved a small fortune over his almost seventy years if he hadn't blindly accepted the bank's first offer. Now you know, too.

Be warned: In bigger banks your negotiating techniques may not work, because these institutions don't believe they need your business. But if that's the case, and you really do have a good credit rating, you should immediately move your accounts to a bank that will appreciate them.

How to Prepare a Winning Financial Statement

At some point in your life you are going to be asked to prepare a personal financial statement. That statement will then be used as one of, or perhaps the only determining factor in the approval or rejection of your loan request.

Many banks require a financial statement with all loan applications over a specific dollar amount, whether the loan is secured or unsecured. A statement is almost always required for loans that are not collateralized.

For nearly all of us a financial statement has little meaning. We fill it out without much thought other than trying to get it over with as soon as possible. That's a mistake. That financial statement is an integral factor in the success or failure of your application. It is imperative that you understand its importance in the lending process. There is a way to prepare a financial statement that will invariably allow for prudent credit to be approved. Here are the specifics.

The first thing I have to warn you about is your friendly loan officer and his or her willingness to assist you in the statement's preparation. If such an offer is made, decline. Take the statement home and prepare it at your own discretion. The reason for this do-it-yourself approach is simple. The loan officer's offer of help is an attempt to help the bank ensure the legitimacy of the figures the statement represents. Its ulterior motive is to stop you from enhancing your net worth. That's almost impossible if the loan officer walks you through the form.

Understand, although the bank doesn't want you to enhance your figures, you want to do exactly that. Statement enhancement is often necessary to receive the fair consideration your request deserves. More on that shortly.

Before proceeding, let me give you the Golden Rule of Financial Statement Preparation: Never lie! To do so in order to secure loan approval is against the law and severely punishable, and, more importantly, it's morally wrong.

Wait a minute. First I tell you to enhance your statement and then I tell you not to lie. Aren't we talking a conflict here? Not really.

Obviously those items on a statement that can be verified must be presented accurately. This includes items like bank account balances, stock ownership, cash surrender value of life insurance, and so on. In case of loan default or bankruptcy, one of the first things a bank does is recheck all submitted documentation, and that includes financial statements. The bank will verify every entry on every form in order to try and prove fraud. That increases its chance of recovery, as evidence of fraud gives it legal leverage. The bank can file a civil law suit or press criminal actions against you. Possibly this will allow it a claim on its insurance policy.

Even if the worst does not occur, a bank financial or regulatory audit may cause you trouble. Examiners and auditors check loan files, and that means they review financial statements. Your odds of getting caught in a lie are high. The penalties are stiff. Frankly, it's not only morally wrong, it's just not worth it.

Are you confused? Don't be. My point will become clear shortly.

Realizing that all verifiable items are not fair game for our task of net-worth enhancement, we're left with the obvious: A financial statement by design is ripe for subjective interpretation. In many cases the bank is asking for our subjective opinion regarding asset worth. This is especially true with your house, personal items, cars, furniture, and the like. This is where we'll get the job done.

Look at the following two examples.

The second form presents a very different, much more positive, financial picture than the first. Yet, we didn't lie to the bank. Those items that are verifiable are completely accurate. Those items that are open to subjective interpretation are reported in a manner favorable to the borrower. Let's examine the differences.

1. *Cash on hand and in banks:* I increased this by $3,000. I'm assuming that this was cash in your possession at the time you prepared the statement that isn't verifiable. Insert whatever is applicable in your case—account for every penny you can lay your hands on.

2. *Real estate owned:* I increased this figure by $20,000. This is my subjective opinion of the value of the house. There is no law that says I have to be a real-estate appraiser. Use some common sense.

3. *Automobiles and personal property:* Here again, the bank asked my opinion. I gave it to them.

4. *Other assets:* This, too, calls for common sense. For this example, I increased the value by $7,500.

FORM I

PERSONAL FINANCIAL STATEMENT

IMPORTANT: Read these directions before completing this Statement

☐ If you are applying for individual credit in your own name and are relying on your own income or assets and not the income or assets of another person as the basis for repayment of the credit requested complete only sections 1 and 3

☐ If you are applying for print credit with another person complete all Sections providing information on Section 2 about the joint applicant

☐ If you are applying for individual credit but are relying on income from alimony, child support, or separate maintenance or on the income of assets of another person as a basis for repayment of the credit requested, complete Sections providing information in Section 2 about the person on whose alimony, support, or maintenance payments or income or assets you are relying

☐ If this statement relates to your guaranty of the indebtedness of other person(s), firm(s), or corporation(s) complete Sections 1 and 3

SECTION 1 - INDIVIDUAL INFORMATION (Type or Print)		SECTION 2 - OTHER PARTY INFORMATION (Type or Print)
Name	John Smith	Name
Residence Address	112 First St.	Residence Address
City, State & Zip	Anywhere, USA	City, State & Zip
Position or Occupation	Foreman	Position or Occupation
Business Name	Smith's Construction	Business Name
Business Address	222 Jones Ln.	Business Address
City, State & Zip	Anywhere, USA	City, State & Zip
Res. Phone 555-3232	Bus. Phone 555-4444	Res. Phone Bus. Phone

SECTION 3 - STATEMENT OR FINANCIAL CONDITION AS OF _____ 19 __

ASSETS (Do not include Assets of doubtful value)	In Dollars (Omit cents)		LIABILITIES	In Dollars (Omit cents)	
Cash on hand and in banks		500	Notes payable to banks - secured	4	500
U.S. Gov't & Marketable Securities - see Schedule A			Notes payable to banks - unsecured		
Non-Marketable Securities - see Schedule B		500	Due to brokers		
Securities held by broker in margin accounts	2	000	Amounts payable to others - secured		
Restricted or control stocks			Amounts payable to others - unsecured		
Partial interest in Real Estate Equities - see Schedule C			Accounts and bills due		
			Unpaid income tax		
Real Estate Owned - see Schedule D	50	000	Other unpaid taxes and interest		
Loans Receivable		500	Real estate mortgages payable see Schedule D	27	500
Automobiles and other personal property	13	000			
Cash value-life insurance-see Schedule E		900	Other debts - itemize		
Other assets - itemize	2	500			
Boat	2	500			
Construction Tools	1	000			
			TOTAL LIABILITIES	32	000
			NET WORTH	38	900
TOTAL ASSETS	70	900	TOTAL LIAB AND NET WORTH	70	900

SOURCES OF INCOME FOR YEAR ENDED _____, 19__		PERSONAL INFORMATION
Salary, bonuses & commisions	$ 24,000.00	Do you have a will? YES If so, name of executor wife
Dividends		Are you a partner or officer in any other venture? If so, describe No
Real estate income		
Other income (Alimony, child support, or separate maintenance		Are you obligated to pay alimony, child support or separate maintenance payments? If so describe
income need not be revealed if you do not wish to have it		No
considered as a basis for repaying this obligation)		
		Are any assets pledged other than as described on schedules? If so describe
TOTAL	$ 24,000.00	No
CONTINGENT LIABILITES		Income tax settled through (date) Current
Do you have any contingent liabilities? If so, describe		Are you a defendant in any suits or legal actions? No
None		Personal bank accounts carried at
As indorser, co-maker or guarantor?	$	1st Natl. Bank
On leases or contracts?	$	
Legal claims	$	Have you ever been declared bankrupt? If so, describe
Other special debt	$	No
Amount of contested income tax liens	$	

(COMPLETE SCHEDULES AND SIGN ON REVERSE SIDE)

PERSONAL FINANCIAL STATEMENT

IMPORTANT: Read these directions before completing this Statement

☐ If you are applying for individual credit in your own name and are relying on your own income or assets and not the income or assets of another person as the basis for repayment of the credit requested complete only sections 1 and 3

☐ If you are applying for print credit with another person complete all Sections providing information on Section 2 about the joint applicant

☐ If you are applying for individual credit but are relying on income from alimony, child support, or separate maintenance or on the income of assets of another person as a basis for repayment of the credit requested, complete Sections providing information in Section 2 about the person on whose alimony, support, or maintenance payments or income or assets you are relying

☐ If this statement relates to your guaranty of the indebtedness of other person(s), firm(s), or corporation(s) complete Sections 1 and 3

SECTION 1 - INDIVIDUAL INFORMATION (Type or Print)		SECTION 2 - OTHER PARTY INFORMATION (Type or Print)	
Name	John Smith	Name	
Residence Address	112 First St.	Residence Address	
City, State & Zip	Anywhere, USA	City, State & Zip	
Position or Occupation	Foreman	Position or Occupation	
Business Name	Smith's Construction	Business Name	
Business Address	222 Jones Ln.	Business Address	
City, State & Zip	Anywhere, USA	City, State & Zip	
Res. Phone 555-3232	Bus. Phone 555-4444	Res. Phone	Bus. Phone

SECTION 3 - STATEMENT OR FINANCIAL CONDITION AS OF _____ 19 __

ASSETS (Do not include Assets of doubtful value)	In Dollars (Omit cents)		LIABILITIES	In Dollars (Omit cents)	
Cash on hand and in banks	3	500	Notes payable to banks - secured	4	500
U.S. Gov't & Marketable Securities - see Schedule A			Notes payable to banks - unsecured		
Non-Marketable Securities - see Schedule B		500	Due to brokers		
Securities held by broker in margin accounts	2	000	Amounts payable to others - secured		
Restricted or control stocks			Amounts payable to others - unsecured		
Partial interest in Real Estate Equities - see Schedule C .			Accounts and bills due		
			Unpaid income tax		
Real Estate Owned - see Schedule D	70	000	Other unpaid taxes and interest		
Loans Receivable		500	Real estate mortgages payable see Schedule D	27	500
Automobiles and other personal property	28	000			
Cash value-life insurance-see Schedule E		900	Other debts - itemize		
Other assets - itemize					
Boat	7	000			
Construction Tools	4	000			
			TOTAL LIABILITIES	32	000
			NET WORTH	84	400
TOTAL ASSETS	116	400	TOTAL LIAB AND NET WORTH	116	400

SOURCES OF INCOME FOR YEAR ENDED _____, 19__		PERSONAL INFORMATION	
Salary, bonuses & commissions	$ 24,000.00	Do you have a will? YES If so, name of executor wife	
Dividends			
Real estate income		Are you a partner or officer in any other venture? If so, describe No	
Other income (Alimony, child support, or separate maintenance income need not be revealed if you do not wish to have it considered as a basis for repaying this obligation)		Are you obligated to pay alimony, child support or separate maintenance payments? If so describe No	
Anticipated Bonus	10,000.00		
TOTAL	$ 34,000.00	Are any assets pledged other than as described on schedules? If so describe No	
CONTINGENT LIABILITIES			
Do you have any contingent liabilities? If so, describe		Income tax settled through (date) Current	
		Are you a defendant in any suits or legal actions? No	
As indorser, co-maker or guarantor?	$	Personal bank accounts carried at 1st Natl. Bank	
On leases or contracts?	$		
Legal claims	$		
Other special debt	$	Have you ever been declared bankrupt? If so, describe No	
Amount of contested income tax liens	$		

(COMPLETE SCHEDULES AND SIGN ON REVERSE SIDE)

You will notice that I also increased the source of income by $10,000. This may not be appropriate for you, but I want to point out all the creative possibilities. This example assumes that your company has some sort of bonus or profit-sharing plan. Assuming that, and assuring that you indicate the money is "anticipated," you may wish to take advantage of increasing your income on the statement. You can't make something like this up, but if there is the slightest chance of additional income, report it.

What have we accomplished through all this? By taking advantage of the leeway in the personal financial statement form, you have become a more desirable loan risk, and a better bank customer in general. It goes hand in hand with creating the image you need to be treated fairly at your bank. It's unfortunate that most banks don't treat their regular customers very well. They reserve prompt loan approval, loan rate concessions, and service charge waivers, for their more affluent customers. By creating a positive image with your financial statement, you will be included in this category.

Let's look at what this preference does to a loan request. For example, assume an unsecured application for $15,000 for four years. Some of the ratios the loan officer will be concerned with are as follows:

Borrowing to net worth:

> Form I = 38.56 %
> Form II = 17.77 %

Repayment percentage of total income for four years:

> Form I = 15.63 %
> Form II = 11.03 %

In each case, the lower the percentage, the better chance of loan approval. The loan becomes more desirable in the lender's eye, because in each case, with Form II, the bank will believe it is more secure. These are the same criteria an examiner would use.

Common sense dictates Form II has a better chance of approval than Form I.

Enhancing your statement is more necessary than ever, now that deregulation has allowed banks to branch out into other towns and states. Now your loan approval or denial may come from a home office far removed from your bank. Those people don't know you. They're number crunchers, and the better you make your numbers look, the better your chances of getting a loan. The point is, in many cases you can't rely on your personal relationships at the bank to get the job done. The people at your bank or branch may have little to say about your loan approval. Even in community banks, many loans are approved by a loan and discount committee. This committee is made up of a few bank officers and a number of bank directors, who may not know you except as a financial statement. This is one of the reasons that Character in the Five Cs of Credit has disappeared. The number crunchers have taken over.

However your bank is set up, you should prepare a financial statement in advance. Complete one now and give it to your banker for your file. Update it every six months whether you use it or not. In this way, you will impress your banker with both your numbers and your apparent knowledge of the inner workings of the bank and the loan department. If you have a favorable statement already on file, your banker will treat you with more respect and consideration. That's human nature.

I would never advocate doing anything illegal or immoral. Yet dealing with the reality of how banks do business sometimes puts my ethics in conflict. Personal financial-statement preparation is one of those areas where this ambivalence comes into play. It is unfortunate that enhancing your statement is necessary, but it is. A person should be able to tell the unvarnished truth and receive fair consideration from a bank. My experience shows that's not the case.

There is one thing to remember about the loan-approval process. No matter what you put down on your financial statement, the loan officer, loan and discount committee, board, home office, or whatever—in an attempt to protect the bank—will discount your reflected net worth by a minimum of 20 percent to 30 percent. That's a fact.

I recommend enhancing your statement, not to take advantage of the bank, but rather so you receive credit for what you would legitimately reflect as your net worth. If you don't enhance, the bank's subsequent actions will deflate your true net worth. If you enhance, you will offset their actions and be back to square one.

Bank statement discounting is called low-balling and all bank officers are familiar with the term. It is universally practiced on many fronts. It is done with financial statements. It is done with property appraisals. You name it, the bank low-balls it. They do so to further protect their equity positions on loans—equity being, in this case, the difference between the loan balance and the value of the loan's collateral. The point is, as subjective as you may be when preparing your statement, I can assure you the bank will be equally so in the opposite direction.

Loan officers cannot make too many mistakes and remain employed. That is why they feel it is to their advantage to be financially conservative in their loan decisions. This is especially true with personal loans. For some reason, banks trust corporations more than individuals. So consumer loan officers believe there isn't any percentage in approving a loan request that isn't solid gold. They don't like marginal credit, or a loan that has an apparent element of risk. One big mistake, or a number of little ones, and the officer will be looking for employment elsewhere. That means we have to set his mind at ease, within the confines of the law and common sense.

Do not forget that some lending is done on a percentage basis. Unsecured loans, for instance, are a reflection of your net worth multiplied by the percentage the bank determines it is willing to lend under those circumstances. Let's say it will loan 30 percent of your net worth unsecured. Knowing that, would you rather present Form I or Form II?

You have to have something going for you in this game. Banks believe they are dealing with a financially uneducated public. In most instances that's true. But because of their low opinion of bank consumers, it's easier to enhance your financial affluence with credibility. Bankers find it hard to believe that a customer knows how to play the game, which makes it easier for us to fight back.

Financial statements carry more weight in the loan decision than they should, but that's the way it is. They are absolutely essential when you are borrowing unsecured money. And when is lending critical? When you don't have collateral, of course.

You are going to need your bankers the most when they are willing to help the least. They are more than willing to help you when you have 100 percent collateral and don't really need the money. On the other hand, when you don't have anything to offer other than your reputation, credit rating, net worth, and other nonliquid assets, you will quickly find out how ruthless your bank can be. That's why you need to plan ahead. Financial statement preparation is one tool at your disposal. If you don't act until you absolutely need the money, it may be too late.

Proper statement preparation can mean an immediate response to lending needs. It can mean the difference between a yes or a no on that important loan application. It may mean the difference between going forward with your business or closing the front doors for good. And that's not taking into account the numerous side benefits that can be realized by creating an affluent image with your bank.

A financial statement, business or personal, looks like an innocuous form. Don't let it fool you. It is designed to deny you credit to which you might otherwise be entitled. By understanding the form's intent, and the thought process of the loan officer, you can beat the odds. You can be continually successful in fulfilling your loan needs.

Since financial success is usually predicated on having money or being able to obtain it, for those who are not blessed with the former, it pays to know ways to accomplish the latter.

Turning No into Yes

Before going into the bad news (what happens when your loan application is turned down), we should review certain specifics that will assist you in receiving a positive response to your loan requests.

First, assuming your loan is viable, there is no reason for your banker to turn you down. A good banking relationship is a two-way street, a fact most bankers have forgotten. The bank wants you on the defensive, because once that is accomplished you will be so happy just to receive loan approval that you would never try to negotiate a better loan rate. Obviously, that is to the bank's advantage. As mentioned, loan rates should be determined by the bank's exposure to risk, with marginal or poor credit customers paying more for the privilege of borrowing. Remember, banks want to charge everyone the same rates and therefore let the good customers, who pay a higher interest rate than they should, pay for the bad customers who become delinquent or default.

This should make it clear that you must negotiate your loan rate. A one-percentage-point rate reduction on the average car loan could save you hundreds of dollars. A one-percentage-point reduction on a $100,000 thirty-year home mortgage will save you roughly $25,000. Even one-half a percentage-point reduction is worth fighting for. When's the last time you saved/made around thirteen thousand dollars for less than an hour's worth of work/negotiation? You can't afford to be intimidated by the bank. You can still find a few institutions that are in business to service the community. Granted, they are becoming hard to find, but, because of the savings that can be accrued, it pays to shop until you find one. Then too, there are alternatives.

It will help your loan request if you'll do some homework in preparing your presentation. Here is where many go wrong. They go into the bank with nothing but themselves, a few figures trusted to memory, and some high hopes. Consistent borrowing success depends on planning. If you have a personal-loan request, make sure you have an updated financial statement with you. Have your figures on the exact cost of the car (or whatever you need a loan to purchase), and know your ratios (what percentage you have put down, and so on). If you have a small-business loan request, you should present a complete package, both business and personal. A large portion of loan denials could be avoided if the customer took time to come to the bank prepared. That will not only help with loan approval, it will also aid in lowering your loan rate.

If your loan is still denied you have two choices. You can try another bank (or one of your many other options), or pursue the matter further with your bank. Assuming you have a history with the bank, most people should opt for the latter. You shouldn't throw away a longstanding banking relationship based on one negative experience. The first thing you should do is approach the loan officer who made the decision and ask why he or she turned you down. Then ask what it would take to elicit a positive response. Often, a loan officer will turn down a request for no substantive reason other than not wanting to be bothered. Yet, when asked to help, the officer will take the time that should have been taken in the first place. Unfortunately, most customers don't follow up a loan denial because they're embarrassed, angry, or think that once the bank has spoken, the decision is final. That's not true.

If the officer won't help, see his or her supervisor. If that doesn't work, go to the president, and if the president won't help, contact the board of directors. As explored earlier, bankers don't like customers going over their heads, and they will do almost anything to avoid that happening, including approving previously rejected loan requests. Over and above that, you may wish to consider other actions outside the bank proper. Consumers having a problem with a bank should review the Appendix under "How to Solve a Problem with Your Bank" (see p. 169).

Of course, you always have the option of a small-claims case against the bank, assuming you have cause. That too is discussed in detail in the Appendix.

Don't forget, you loan your bank money every day. That's what your deposits are, a loan to the bank. The truth is, depositors loan the bank more money each day than the bank loans to its customers, so it would follow that the relationship should flow fairly in both directions.

Come to the loan interview prepared with documentation and a positive attitude. If your original request is denied, don't be afraid to pursue the matter further within the bank. If you're still unsuccessful, you have regulatory and legal options that are simple and direct—and more importantly, usually force immediate action by the bank.

Once you learn how the bank plays the game, you will always be able to borrow money for any worthwhile reason, and at interest rates far below what most would think possible.

Installment Loans

Installment Loans

Once you know your loan has been approved and you're satisfied with the interest rate, you must pay attention to the loan vehicle and its associated paperwork. The most common type of personal loan offered to individual bank customers is the installment loan. An installment loan is a loan whereby the customer pays a portion of the value of the loan each month until the amount owed is completely amortized (paid). Not surprisingly, it is not consumer friendly. Because of that, if at all possible, you should never borrow money on an installment-loan basis.

Let's look at a car loan where the car has a value of $12,000 and you make a down payment of $2,000. That leaves you with a balance of $10,000. For this example, I will use an interest rate of 10.25 percent annual percentage rate (APR). A 10.25 APR is the use-of-money equivalent of a 5.58 percent add-on rate. (Note: This rate was chosen as representative of most recent market conditions.)

Sample Car Loan

10.25% APR for 48 months

Principal	$10,000.00
Credit Life	270.07
Disability insurance	769.69
Amount financed	11,039.76
Finance charge	2,463.60
Total due	13,503.36
Monthly payments	$281.32

These are the conditions that your bank is most likely to offer you. They will not give you alternatives, just this one option, because it garners them the best return.

Let's go back. Remembering that the cost of the car was $12,000, we can see the real cost exceeds the original value by $3,503.36 (loan total of $13,503.36 plus our down payment of $2,000 minus the price tag of $12,000). Not a very good way of amassing a net worth, is it? It is important for you always to think in terms of the total transaction.

The question now is, how can you improve this loan position and save money in the process? First of all, never buy credit life and disability insurance from the lender. This is discussed in-depth in the next section. I included these in the example because virtually all banks will write the insurance into the loan contract regardless of your wants and needs. Let's rewrite the example deleting those charges.

Sample Car Loan

10.25% APR for 48 months	
Principal	$10,000.00
Credit life	.00
Disability insurance	.00
	————
Amount financed	10,000.00
Finance charge	2,231.36
	————
Total due	12,231.36
Monthly payments	$254.82

We've saved $26.50 a month, or $1,272 over the whole term of the loan. But there are more savings to be found.

Never forget, installment loans are front-end loaded, that is, you are charged the interest rate multiplied by the original balance throughout the term of the loan. Many borrowers are confused on this point (i.e., they believe that at the halfway point of the loan that they are paying interest only on 50 percent of what was borrowed. That isn't true. You are paying interest, in our example loan, on $10,000 for each and every month of the loan's term).

Why isn't there a decreasing correlation between the interest rate and the declining balance? Because banks are more than willing to increase their profits at your expense. They are happy to arrange financing that isn't understood by the customer. Most of us rely on the bank or banker to help us with our lending needs, but unfortunately this is when the banker acts to his own advantage. It is up to you, then, to secure more favorable conditions for your loan.

Let's see if we can turn this loan around and reduce our costs even further.

When you go to your bank and receive loan approval and a percentage rate, tell your banker that you will accept the rate and term but that you want to borrow on a *simple-interest single-payment note* that allows for monthly payments—which means that each monthly payment is calculated on the declining principal instead of on the original balance. (Some banks offer installment loans that are calculated on a simple-interest basis. This is an acceptable alternative. Make sure to ask.) Many banks will make statements to the effect that they don't make loans in that manner or form. That's a lie. They do so all the time. What they really mean is they don't want to make that type of loan to you. If that's their response, it's time to change banks. You can't afford to do business with them any longer.

It should be obvious that if your banker approved your loan at X percent, over a specified term, it shouldn't matter what form the loan takes unless there is something they're not telling you. There is: They want to take more of your money through the simple deception of failing to inform you of all your financial options.

An installment loan works for the bank and against the customer for only one reason: The inequity of government supervision allows banks the right to use varying methods of interest computation, which means that all things that look equal may not be.

Let me make the point clearer. Surely you would agree that a 10.25 percent APR is a 10.25 percent APR no matter how you look at it. Not so! In our example loan your original finance charge was $2,463.69. We reduced this to $2,231.36 by eliminating credit life and disability insurance and the associated charge to finance the premium. So far we have reduced your expense by 9.4 percent. Now let's compute the loan on a simple interest, single-payment note basis with forty-eight monthly payments. Your monthly payments would be $208.33 ($10,000 divided by forty-eight months) plus a declining monthly interest expense. The total interest paid over the loan's term is now $2,092.49.

How can a 10.25 percent APR not be a 10.25% APR? The interest rate is the same in each case. The amount borrowed is the same. The loan's term is the same. The difference is the method of interest computation. This little bit of consumer deception is one of a bank's major income producers.

Simply by asking for a different note, you'll have saved

$138.87—that's 6.2 percent. Add this to our prior savings and you have reduced your expense 15.6 percent. Now let's look at the actual dollar savings:

Credit life insurance	$270.07
Disability insurance	769.69
Cost of financing insurance	228.74
Difference between installment and single payment note	138.87
Total savings	$1,407.37

Some other factors accrue in this borrowing technique. On the installment basis, your payments were $254.82 throughout the loan's term. On the single-payment note basis, at the same interest rate, your payment would be $293.74 for the first month, $252.81 for the twenty-fourth month, and $210.27 for the last month. You would not only have saved money in total interest expense, you would have constantly improved your monthly cash flow.

My example is conservative. Most new cars cost more than our example. In short, your savings will probably grossly exceed the savings shown.

This loan-interest saving technique is applicable to any lending situation. What's important, in addition to shopping for the lowest interest rate, is that you demand your financial option borrowing on something other than an add-on, installment-loan basis. Do this after the banker has committed to a rate, however, because if you tip your hand before then he or she will simply adjust the rate higher, which in effect will offset your savings.

Apart from the additional interest expense associated with installment loans, they have the added drawback of locking you in once the loan is signed. The reason for this is the Rule of 78s, which is the method the bank uses to accelerate the interest into their profit account.

Without getting too technical, the Rule of 78s means in principle that approximately 75 percent of the loan's interest has been paid to the bank by the halfway point of the loan. Ninety percent of the interest has been paid at the three-quarters mark, and so on. This means that if you try to pay off the loan early you will not receive a true reimbursement or rebate. Why? Because you paid substantial interest before it was actually due.

Let me give you an example.

These figures are from an actual case of a person who took out a forty-eight-month installment loan. After making six monthly payments, he decided to pay off the balance. He was amazed at the payoff figure because of how much he had already paid into the account. The original loan breakdown was as follows:

Principal	$15,000.00
Credit life	544.50
Disability insurance	816.75
	————
Total financed	16,361.25
Interest	4,581.15
	————
Total	$20,942.40
Monthly payments	$436.30
Payments made during six months	$2,617.80
Payoff figure from bank at end of six months	$13,761.65

The customer wanted to know how the payoff figure could be so high. The payoff figure plus his previously made payments totalled $16,379.45. He borrowed only $15,000 for six months at an APR of 12.68 percent (the equivalent of a 7 percent add-on rate), and the interest for that period (on a simple-interest basis) should have been only $525. He was sure the bank had made an error. Unfortunately, the bank hadn't made the error, the customer had. He should never have borrowed money on an installment basis. He should not have bought credit life and disability insurance.

Remember, when you borrow on an installment loan you are

borrowing the interest too. That's not the case with a simple interest, single-payment note. That's why the original balance this customer owed totalled $20,942.40. He didn't realize it, but he borrowed the principal, the money to purchase the credit life insurance, the money to purchase the disability insurance, and the interest in advance. That's why he paid $2,617.80 and still owed $13,761.65. This is how the Rule of 78s works. That's how you get locked in to paying additional interest if you try to pay off the typical installment loan early.

Let's review and compare the real cost to this customer, and what he should have paid.

Installment loan actual interest cost	$1,379.45

Cost if note had been a
    single payment, simple-
    interest note
	$525.00

	———
Difference (loss)	$854.45

Actual net interest
    rate cost for installment
    loan (due to early payoff)
	18.36%

Interest rate for simple
    interest note (as expressed
    in add-on rate)
	7.00%

Difference (loss)	11.35%

Since installment loans are front-end loaded, your net cost is greatly increased should you pay your loan off earlier than at term. In this case, had the customer used a single payment, simple-interest note, he would have saved a substantial sum, as there is no penalty for paying off that note early. In fact, by choosing the wrong type of loan, this customer paid well over 100 percent of what the loan should have cost in interest.

Borrowing on installment will cost you thousands you should not have spent, and lock you into a situation where there is a penalty for paying off the loan early.

Never forget these important facts, which bankers try to hide and most people never fully understand. Knowing how to borrow money is just as important as knowing how and where to invest your savings.

Credit Life and Disability Insurance

In the last section I discussed how to effectively reduce your borrowing expense. One aspect of that discussion was the principle that you shouldn't purchase credit life and disability insurance from a bank, or any lender for that matter. Let me explain why.

Credit life insurance is insurance offered through the lender that will pay the lender the balance of your loan liability should you die. In short, the insurer pays the bank the balance of the loan at the time of your death. Obviously, then, what you are purchasing is a rapidly decreasing term policy, as most installment loans have terms of forty-eight months or less. Additionally, some policies have exceptions for suicides, death that occurs within a predetermined time after signing the loan, and so on. The actual coverage may vary with each insurer. Disability insurance is also offered through the lender and guarantees your monthly loan payment will be made should you become disabled and unable to work. Usually, you must buy the credit life insurance before you can buy the disability insurance.

Of course, like most insurance policies, credit life and disability are written in "insurancese" for the purpose of selling something other than what the consumer believes he is buying. And the cost is higher than most realize.

Let's go back to our example loan.

Principal	$10,000.00
Credit life insurance	270.07
Disability insurance	769.69
Amount financed	11,039.76
Finance charge	2,463.60
Total due	$13,503.36
Monthly payments	$281.32

Remember, this example is for forty eight-months at 10.25 percent APR (5.58 percent add-on rate).

The total cost for the credit life and disability insurance is $1,039.76. That is equal to 10.4 percent of the principal. It represents 7.7 percent of the total loan. That means that in this example, you are going to make 3.69 payments just for the insurance coverage. If this were a joint loan and you purchased joint coverage, the cost would be even higher.

If you check the last section, you will see that without the insurance coverage your loan payments are reduced to $254.82. That's a monthly savings of $26.50, or 9.4 percent. You would have reduced your total owed to the bank by $1,272. Best of all—and this is what most fail to realize and lenders conveniently fail to mention—you have reduced your finance charge. Why? Because the lender makes the insurance premium part of the loan itself and therefore, because you're borrowing the premium's cost, it is subject to a finance charge.

The cost of the loan insurance in our example is $1,039.76 ($270.07 + $769.69). The hidden cost is the difference between the two examples' finance charges, or $232.24 ($2,463.60 − $2,231.36). You won't find that amount on the loan contract. Clearly, this example illustrates that the current Truth in Lending law is not offering the consumer adequate loan disclosure. That added hidden expense represents additional finance-charge costs of 9.4 percent. It increases the true cost of the insurance alone by 22.3 percent ($232.24 ÷ $1,039.76).

The real cost of the insurance, then, is $1,272 ($1,039.76 + $232.24). You won't find that figure on the loan form, either.

Earlier I mentioned that the insurance cost represented 10.4 percent of the principal. With the finance charge, that figure jumps to 12.7 percent.

The real crux of the issue is that the customer isn't purchasing what he thinks he is purchasing. Neither credit life or disability insurance, as used in this context, insures the consumer. They insure the lender. In the case of credit life insurance, if you die, the check will be issued and sent to the bank for the sole purpose of paying the bank the loan's remaining balance. It may be more beneficial for your family to take the monies, use them for other needs, and continue to make the monthly payments as agreed. But, the money is not theirs to take. It belongs to the bank. All you have done by purchasing credit life insurance is relieve the bank from its responsibility of collecting on a possible debt problem due to the death of one of their borrowers. Remembering the Rule of 78s, this insurance early payoff actually increases the bank's net return on your loan. The bank profits in two ways, both at your expense.

That notwithstanding, you should realize that credit life insurance is a bet between you and the insurer that you will die before paying off the loan. (The bank is not the insurer; it is an agent of the insurance company.) It is a bad bet for the consumer, and the bank and the insurance company know it.

In fact, credit life is a major bank money-maker. Though banks and insurance companies are reluctant to disclose exact figures, it is generally agreed that credit life payouts total less than 3 percent of the premiums collected. That ought to give you a rough idea of how valuable the policy is to you and your family. Statistically, it's worthless. To the bank, it's a gold mine.

Disability insurance is another matter. Banks and the insurer know that even though the odds are remote that any payout will be necessary, the chances are better that you will become disabled than they are that you will die during the loan's term. Hence the larger premium for disability insurance. Disability claims are routinely denied, by the way, as there are many policy exceptions.

These policies are, in most cases, sold without proper documentation or a chance for the consumer to read and understand what he is buying. The actual policy is often mailed to the purchaser days or weeks after the loan has been signed. You've spent hundreds of dollars—perhaps thousands on very large loans—on a policy you have yet to read, and because you receive your policy through the mails the chances are you will never read it until it's too late. That delay is planned by the bank and the insurer for that very reason. They don't want you to make an intelligent financial decision, and by once again withholding vital information, they have accomplished that goal.

For instance, they won't tell you that you can buy the policy outright, thereby avoiding the finance charge. They just include it in the loan form in an effort to drive up your costs.

Lending officers in most banking institutions are taught how to sell credit life and disability insurance. The principal ploy used—and note the sexist nature of the tactic—is to "sell the wife." Lending officers are taught to frighten nonworking wives with the thought of having to pay the bills if her husband passes on. Using this tactic, the bank usually has very little trouble making the sale.

An even better technique routinely employed is to ensure that there is no discussion about the policy at all. The lender simply types the insurance information into the loan papers. The first time the customer even sees or hears about the premiums and their cost is at the loan closing, and then they are glossed over. The customer normally accepts the added cost for fear that, at this late stage, he or she could lose the loan by rocking the boat.

Still other customers simply don't understand the loan forms at all. They are the perfect fodder for the bank's insurance abuse.

Often, banks will tell you that credit life and disability insurance are required before they can make you a consumer loan. Except in rare cases in certain states, this is not true, and requiring them is a violation of law. Yet this practice is routine at some banks. The lender cannot force you to take insurance coverage, and if the loan is denied on that basis, you may have the makings of a lawsuit, perhaps a class-action suit.

Why are banks anxious to sell you insurance? Why else but profits? Although they won't tell you this, the lender (bank) gets an immediate 40 percent kickback from the insurer (insurance company) for making the sale.

Here again the bank is withholding information that you need to make the right financial decision. When you deal with an insurance agent, you know he is making money by selling you your purchase—that is obvious on its face. The relationship between your money, the agent, and the insurance company is understood. However, when we purchase insurance from a bank, the relationship is purposely confused and muted. There is a blatant conflict of interest that is hidden from your review.

When you purchase insurance through the bank, the bank is the beneficiary, you pay 100 percent of the premium plus additional charges to finance the premium, and the lender pockets a 40 percent kickback under the table. In our sample loan, it would mean that the bank pocketed $415.90 for doing absolutely nothing for you.

Let's go back to what you have actually purchased. With credit life, you own an accelerated term policy. Term insurance is normally a good buy, but not under these circumstances. In our example loan, the real cost for the policy, taking everything into account, was $1,272. That's 4.52 payments just to cover the premiums plus interest cost, or approximately 10 percent of your total monthly payments due. That's quite a bit, yet the "benefits" disappear rapidly.

Bank Credit Life Insurance

Amount of original coverage	$13,503.36
After 24 months	6,751.68
After 36 months	3,375.84
Cost of coverage	$329.48
($270.07 + $59.41 finance charge)	

If you are determined to purchase a policy, you could purchase a whole-life policy for the term of the loan from your local insurance agent. I called one, and was quoted a policy for a 35-year-old person, face value of $13,503.36, for four years at a full cost of $216. Let's look at this from a comparison standpoint.

Life Insurance Through Agent

Amount of coverage for full 48 months	$13,503.36
Cost of coverage	$216.00

This gives you a savings of $113.48 ($329.48 − $216.00). For two-thirds the cost, you are covered for the full amount of the loan for the entire term. Clearly, you can use your own agent for more coverage at less cost. In other words, if something should happen later in the loan's term, let's say at the thirty-six-month mark, your "benefit" from the bank is going to be $3,375.84. Through the insurance agent it will still be $13,503.36.

Disability insurance is another matter entirely. This type of individual coverage is hard to purchase through an insurance agent because of its prohibitive cost. Yet, many of you probably have some disability coverage through your employer. Further, should the disability become severe, you have Workman's Compensation and Social Security. For most it is safe to say purchasing bank disability insurance is simply buying something you already have.

For those of you who aren't covered elsewhere, bank disability insurance is still a bad buy. Within the policy's requirements (an important point), it will only make payments for that time you are unable to work. Remember, you have to buy credit life before you can purchase disability, so it's true, full cost is hidden or ignored by many. Using that criterion, however, means that in our example loan, you would have to be totally disabled for almost five months just to break even on the original premium. When was the last time you were disabled for five months?

No matter what the exact figures or conditions are, there's an important principle to remember. When you buy bank credit life and disability insurance, you are locking yourself in. Your family can use the money for only one purpose, repaying the loan. But how can you know in advance what your family's priorities will be in the event of your death or disability?

Again, never buy credit life insurance or disability insurance. They are grossly overpriced. They offer less coverage for your family than you could purchase on your own. They insure the lender at your expense. The lender receives a 40 percent hidden payment that comes directly out of your pocket. The real net insurance cost, including the finance charge for the premium, is hidden from your review. If you feel the need for extra security, consider purchasing additional life insurance.

One final, sobering note: Many bankers privately refer to credit life and disability insurance as "our license to steal." Unfortunately, they're right.

Loan Late Charges

The lending function is one of a bank's most important services. That's why I've discussed installment lending in depth. There is, however an added aspect of that function that needs to be reviewed: loan late charges.

As you know, banks assess a late charge for loan payments that are delinquent more than ten days. The ten days constitutes a grace period. In most instances the late charge is fifteen dollars. Bankers say that they have to charge a late fee, as they lose money when a customer is tardy with his obligation. There are computer costs, personnel expenses, loss of interest revenue. That sounds fair. After all, banks shouldn't have to incur a loss because a customer doesn't meet a commitment. We can all agree to that.

However, I believe a closer review shows conclusively that loan late charges are excessive and unfair.

First, let's look at the charge itself. As a banker, I acknowledge the bank shouldn't have to lose money because a customer fails to make a payment when he or she agreed to do so—but that's where other bankers and I part company. The bank should be able to recoup only its expense, as it is already being paid substantial interest from the loan itself. And what are the bank's expenses? As an example, let's review a $250 payment that is fifteen days past due.

Bank Expenses

Computer cost	$.25
Mailing (postage and envelope)	.34
Investment loss to bank (average loss on $250 for 15 days)	1.33
Employee expense (5 minutes at $6 per hour)	.50
Total	$2.42

In all fairness, I can tell you that I am being generous in this analysis. For instance, it doesn't take five minutes to process a delinquent loan notice, and most low-level staff bookkeeping people at community banks don't make six dollars per hour. For balance, I am understating my case. Now let's review the bank's revenue from the late charge.

Bank's Profit

Bank fee to customer	$15.00
Less expenses	2.42
Net profit	$12.58

They spend $2.42 and make $12.58. That's a return of 520 percent. I believe "excessive" aptly describes their fee.

Now to the question of fairness.

Forget the figures above, even though they are undeniably incriminating, and perhaps by themselves prove the late charge is unfair. There is an even better way to judge. If the bank assesses customers a charge for being late with their monthly loan payments, then, in fairness, it should be willing to pay them fifteen dollars when they make their payment ten days early. Reversing the bank's logic for assessing a late charge, an early payment means that the bank gets to reinvest your payment earlier than anticipated, and for that you should be compensated.

Does your bank have an early loan-payment bonus? Of course not. As usual, banks have one policy for themselves and another for the customer. In each and every case, the bank profits excessively and unfairly at your expense.

MORTGAGE LOANS

Shop, Shop, and Shop for the Best Deal

Your mortgage will probably be the largest loan you ever sign for, so it follows that finding the lowest interest rate is extremely important.

I'm not going to take a lot of time discussing this because we've already covered loan-rate negotiations. Instead, I'm going to let a few quick examples reinforce my point.

On the standard $100,000, thirty-year mortgage, a one-percentage point reduction in interest rate—whether it's from 12 percent to 11 percent, 9 percent to 8 percent, or something else—saves the borrower over $25,000 over the term of the loan. A half a percentage point saves almost $13,000. Even a quarter of a percentage point saves more than $6,000.

You see, even a quarter of a percentage point is worth fighting for. When's the last time you made between $6,000 and $25,000 for a few hours of shopping and negotiating? If you have an answer to that, congratulations, you're making a lot more money than I am.

The point is—most people don't understand this, and your banker won't tell you—a small percentage increase applied to a large sum of money over an extended period of time means a great deal of profit to the bank. Conversely, even a small interest-rate reduction means a great deal of profit (or savings) to you.

Unfortunately, small rate variations seem harmless, but as you can see, they're not. By understanding what the banks under-stand, you may save—again, with very little work—enough to send one of your kids to college. Or, you can ignore my advice, pay the higher rate, and send one of your banker's kids to college.

How to Find the Best Mortgage

Because a home is most families' biggest investment, they spend a great deal of time locating the property that will best suit their needs. Unfortunately, while finding the right home is important, perhaps more important to your finances is finding the right mort-gage. Seldom does that requirement receive the amount of time and effort it deserves. Most families talk to just one bank—their usual bank, or the one institution the real-estate agent recom-mends. That's a costly mistake.

What should you be looking for? Obviously, you should be concerned with the amount of money you are going to spend acquiring the loan, but remember that the real savings are to be gained by lowering your mortgage interest rate. Any reduction is worth fighting for, as outlined previously. Remember, we are not talking about insignificant amounts of money. The question is, Are you going to pay the bank in the form of added interest, or pay yourself in the form of savings?

One of the ways you can shop for the best mortgage is to use a mortgage-reporting service. These firms survey a minimum of two major lenders in most market areas every week and then publish information on which firms are offering mortgage money and on what terms. The cost for the service is approximately twenty-five dollars—cheap when you consider the savings they may be able to locate. Many real-estate agencies use these firms, so if you ask, your agent may let you look at their reports for free. In addition to saving you time, the main benefit is that their reports will give you information on financial institutions outside your market that are willing to loan money in your geographical area. This is an acknowledgment that many of the best mortgage deals are available outside of where you and your agent would normally look. If the deal's to your advantage, you shouldn't care where the money comes from, just that the price is right. This service is also valuable for those in the process of remortgaging.

Here are a few firms that offer listings in more than one state:

HSH Associates
Ten Mead Avenue
Riverdale, NJ 07457
(201) 831–0550 or (800) 873–2837
Surveys in more than thirty states, with contacts at approximately 2,000 institutions.

National Mortgage Weekly
P.O. Box 18081
Cleveland, OH 44118
(216) 371–2767
Surveys Detroit, Boston, Columbus, and Cleveland.

Peeke LoanFax, Inc.
101 Chestnut Street, Suite 200
Gaithersburg, MD 20877
(301) 840–5752
Surveys Washington, D.C., Virginia; Maryland; Baltimore; and Broward, Dade, and Palm Beach counties in Florida, as well as Miami and Fort Lauderdale.

Gary Meyers and Associates
20 West Hubbard Street, Suite 500
Chicago, IL 60610
(312) 670–2440
Surveys numerous markets. Call for their rapidly expanding market area listing.

Other, more local, services are available. Call your bank and see if they know of firms in your area. Ask your real estate broker. They may be able to put you in contact with firms not on my list. Perhaps the best deal can be garnered from a combination of an outside firm's listing and your own efforts. In my consulting work

I am amazed how often, when reviewing this subject with a client, I hear something like this: "But I don't have the time to shop for a mortgage. We're moving. I have to work. I really don't want to spend an extra twenty-five dollars for a report," and so on. My answer to that is, with the amount of money involved, how can you afford *not* to shop for the best mortgage? Because of the money involved, mortgage shopping is something you must do regardless of any inconvenience.

Too many homeowners are victims of a misunderstanding of numbers and how they work in a lending transaction. One percentage point sounds so harmless. Certainly a half a point does. But, as I've shown, when expressed in dollars over the term of a mortgage, tiny percentages amount to a great deal. That's why you have to shop, shop, and shop until you find the least expensive, best deal available. Chances are, your shopping will reveal that your bank's terms were among the worst.

Adjustable Rate Mortgages—You Could Wake Up to Find You Can No Longer Afford Your Home

An important aspect of mortgage borrowing is knowing which loan vehicle is best under the greatest number of circumstances. In most cases you have the choice of either a fixed or adjustable rate mortgage (ARM). In some parts of the country an ARM is called a variable rate mortgage. No matter what they are called, you must avoid them! ARMs are not usually in your best interest (although there may be isolated instances when for certain people an ARM makes sense) because they are designed solely for the purpose of added bank profits. And added bank profits means added consumer expense. They protect the bank from free-market forces and you pay the cost.

The old, recommended mortgage agreement is the fixed-rate loan. Once you signed the documentation, your interest rate was guaranteed to remain the same as long as you decided to stay at that residence. Your rate was known and could not change without your permission, and although your escrow account might increase with your taxes and the like, the principal and interest remained the same. Then came adjustable rate mortgages.

Their name indicates exactly what they are. The interest rate is adjustable, and depending on the trigger mechanism the bank uses, your monthly payment amount could change dramatically numerous times throughout its term. Some of these loans have a cap on them, others don't. Some have a cap on the number of changes allowed, others don't. The terms of these loans are varied, but the effect on your payments is not.

Let's look at an example that shows what rate adjustments can do to a $100,000 ARM with a thirty-year term:

ARM Adjustments

Additional Percentage Points	Added Total Repayment
1	$25,509.60
2	51,771.60
3	78,681.60
4	106,146.00
5	134,074.80

These kinds of increases may mean you can lose your home, because the monthly expenditures become too large for the family budget. Why the ARMs? Banks have decided, in concert I might add, that keeping the mortgage rates at roughly 3 percent over the inflation rate (the historic industry benchmark) is no longer generating enough income. They then artificially dried up the mortgage market (made mortgage money tight) in order to convince the public that they, the banks, needed to be isolated from market forces, such as inflation. They want you to pay continually for their cost of doing business. They also like making a huge income from the safest loan possible, a home mortgage.

But what happens if rates go down? Won't you save money? Possibly. But not at the same rate you stand to lose money. Remember, bankers control interest rates. When rates go up they go up rapidly. When rates go down, they do so slowly. It is safe to assume that for every dollar you might save with an ARM, you will pay it back and more sometime over your mortgage term. Then, too, if you have a fixed-rate mortgage, if rates do go down you can remortgage. The important thing is, with a fixed rate your payments can't go up. With an adjustable-rate mortgage you're speculating with your home—and that's dangerous.

ARMs mean that the consumer is often paying more for mortgage money than commercial loan customers do, customers who are more often a riskier proposition. Here, the bankers have the best of both worlds. Overcharge the consumer on one of the safest loans, a home mortgage, and use those exaggerated profits for what amounts to speculation in other lending areas—for example, the Third World.

Bankers lobbied for deregulation under the premise that it would be good for the consumer. They said the customer would benefit in the loan arena by a decline in interest rates due to increased competition. But as soon as they got congressional deregulation approval, ARMs went full bore, which, in effect, then protected the banks from deregulation in the mortgage market. Financially clever, but unfair and costly to the consumer.

As a mortgage customer you should never enter into any mortgage agreement unless it is a fixed-rate loan. It may be slightly more costly up front (another banking repackaging gimmick), but it will pay for itself in cost and peace of mind.

Of course, almost all banks are now encouraging ARMs. So what? Never forget there are other avenues for all your lending needs. Do your business elsewhere if you're being financially abused.

Another ARM problem involves overcharging when interest rates change and your mortgage is recalculated. Independent surveys indicate that up to 80 percent of ARMs have been recalculated incorrectly. It's estimated that these overcharges may total billions of dollars nationwide. It defies credulity to think that's just an honest mistake. Banks have the best calculating equipment made, and as bankers are always telling us when they screw up our accounts, "Our computers don't make mistakes." Taking them at their word means the overcharges (pure profit to the bank) are done on purpose. Don't hold your breath if you're waiting for government to step in and force the banks to repay those overcharged. Better to hire an independent mortgage-audit firm. Some charge a fee only if they can recover money for you.

One final thought on the subject of ARMs. Banks convinced the public that ARMs are "fair" because banks shouldn't be locked in to a lower interest rate when rates have escalated. History suggests otherwise. For decades, banks made fixed-rate mortgages and profited handsomely all the while, even in times of severe double-digit inflation. ARMs have nothing to do with fairness. Added profits is the bottom line. If fairness of rate was really the issue, banks would offer us increased or sliding savings rates, but most don't. If you have a certificate of deposit for five years at 6 percent does the bank give you 9 percent if savings rates increase to that level? Not normally. You can withdraw your money after paying a penalty, but the bank on its own usually offers the depositor nothing when interest rates increase. As always, the goal is more bank profit, and we know who pays for that.

If you have any doubt that an ARM is a dangerous way to borrow, go back to the ARM adjustments chart on page 97 and see what added expense you'll accrue with each percentage point increase. When an increase happens, you don't receive any more money, a better home, or any benefit whatsoever. All you get is added expense.

Closing Costs = Expense and, Often, Hidden Fees

When you apply for a mortgage loan at most banks you will be assessed an application fee, usually fifty dollars to seventy-five dollars. If your application is acceptable the bank proceeds with a credit check, costing fifty dollars to one hundred dollars. If you pass the credit check, the bank requires an appraisal of the property you want to buy, for approximately three hundred dollars. If that meets their standards, you need a title search, an attorney—and are charged a few other bank filing charges as well. Usually these total $1,000 to $1,500. Assuming the bank is still willing to make the loan, you are then presented a "points" bill of 2 to 4 percent of the amount of the mortgage. On a $100,000 mortgage, you are looking at two to four thousand dollars. In total, it's very easy to have costs of five to six thousand dollars on the average home mortgage—and that's before you make your first payment.

Points are fees you have to pay the bank for the privilege of borrowing mortgage money that is probably overpriced already. Let's dissect each charge:

1. *Application fee:* Banks have us so bullied that they aren't afraid to demand money before they will even make a service effort to look at our application. Application fees are an excellent example of the arrogance of modern bankers. Application fees should be a cost-of-doing-business expense of the bank.

2. *Credit check fee:* This, too, is a fee that should not be borne by the customer. If the bank wants to establish your credit character, they should pay for it. Worse yet, the amount they charge is often far in excess of what they are charged by the credit bureau(s) they contact, so not only are you expected to pay the cost, you are expected to offer the bank a hidden profit.

3. *Appraisal fee:* The appraisal of the property offered as collateral is done either by the bank staff or someone they hire. It's the bank's method of ensuring there is enough collateral equity to protect their position in case of default.

But as for loan fees, let's examine the hows and whys. The borrowers don't profit from the appraisal. They have already offered to buy the property, so it's assumed they know the relative value of the home. No, as with the above fees, an appraisal is ordered and used by the bank. The customer has little to gain from the bank's appraisal, as it based on the bank's assessment of loan value as opposed to market value. And yes, this too is your expense.

Once again, the bank often makes money on the appraisal. A standard home-mortgage appraisal done by a bank employee familiar with the area takes no more than an hour. The profit to the bank is obvious. If it hires an outside appraiser, the fee is usually split fifty-fifty.

4. *Title search, attorney, etc.:* All home sales and closings need a title search. That's for your protection and that of the bank. Unfortunately, even though both have need of the service, the borrower pays 100 percent of the cost.

If you have an attorney present at the closing—something I strongly recommend—you should pay his or her bill. However, you should not have to pay the bank's attorney, as is done at many institutions.

On the subject of handling and filing fees I have strong objections. Like the application fee, this is part of the bank's cost of doing business. Every service-oriented business has costs that it has to bear. Banks are one of the few service industries that believe they should make a substantial profit every time one of their staff lifts a finger to help a customer.

5. *Points:* These represent an arbitrary fee assessed by the bank for doing absolutely nothing. They are not satisfied with the high cost of a mortgage and all the fees they have collected to this point; they want more. "Closing costs" on the average mortgage are two to four thousand dollars. This is nothing more than additional bank profit.

One litmus test for any service charge is whether or not it is based on a cost analysis or sliding scale. A cost-analysis approach allowing for a reasonable profit is fair. A sliding scale is not. Points fail the test as they are assessed on a percentage basis. If a bank charges three points to close a $100,000 mortgage, the cost is $3,000. A $200,000 mortgage costs $6,000. But—and here is the cost analysis—whatever the actual expense, assuming the bank actually spends one dollar on your behalf, it costs the same to put a $100,000 mortgage on the books as it does a one-million-dollar mortgage. Points aren't a fair assessment of anything anyway. The sliding scale exacerbates the abuse.

Let's take this further to see another important point. Because of points, and the way they are reported to the borrower, chances are your mortgage annual percentage rate is understated. Closing costs should be figured into the loan's true APR and reported to the borrower. Points of $3,000 on a $100,000 mortgage at 9 percent for thirty years raises the APR to 9.12 percent.

But even that representation is not accurate. Statistics show that the average home is sold every three years (approximately) and your banker knows the statistic well. Let's use a conservative five years to make the point. If that three thousand dollars is applied to the same mortgage over a five-year span, the true APR jumps more than one-half percentage point. Assuming your mortgage is reflective of the norm, that's an unreported 7.6 percent increase in the true cost of your mortgage.

Your bank has done nothing illegal here, except that it's fair once again to challenge the integrity of a supposedly friendly financial institution preparing documentation it well knows more than likely understates your true costs. This trend also makes clear that present consumer protection laws are inadequate.

Reviewing this policy in actual dollars makes the point clearer. If your mortgage were to run to term, three thousand dollars in points costs one hundred dollars per year ($3,000 ÷ 30 years). The same three thousand dollars costs one thousand dollars per year if your home is sold in three years; six hundred dollars per year if it's sold in five years, and so on. Unless you stay in that house for the loan's term, your APR is not reflective of your actual expense.

Mortgage closing costs form another excellent example of why you must shop your loan needs. We discussed earlier and will discuss again later how expensive a home mortgage can be if not aggressively negotiated; but, as you can see, it's not with just the loan itself we have to be concerned. The associated fees alone are worth shopping for, as they have a substantial impact on your true mortgage expense. You not only have to shop and negotiate your loan rate, you must shop and negotiate your loan fees.

These tips will help:

1. Many banks will waive their application fee if you ask, especially if you're a current bank customer.

2. Instead of paying an exorbitant credit-check fee, go to the credit bureau directly and request your report (cost: about twenty dollars) and then hand it to your banker, thereby saving their middleman cost.

3. Talk to the bank about the appraiser—find one on whom you can both agree and then hire that person and pay the bill directly, once again cutting the bank out of its middleman profit.

4. Just in case the bank is tacking on an added fee for the title search, tell your banker that you'll want to pay the title company with a separate check, so you'll need to see the bill as opposed to a bank statement—or, go the title company yourself, pay the bill, and forward the report to the bank.

5. Never pay for the bank's attorney. While doing so is not necessarily illegal, it does present a clear conflict of interest that your bank will quite possibly "understand" if you bring the issue to its attention.

6. Points are the biggest expense, so much of your shopping effort should be directed here. What is obtainable through negotiation or by playing one bank against the other is a reduction in points of 30 percent to 50 percent.

There are too many options today for anyone to get beaten in a mortgage loan, but almost everyone does. It's as if people walk into their bank, throw their wallets on the banker's desk, and say, "Here, take what you need." Fortunately, you're not going to do that.

More Deception—Points Versus Rate

In addition to locating the right home and mortgage lender, consumers are now faced with another problem: Which is better, a lower interest rate or lower closing costs?

This question has become an issue in the last few years. It used to be a mortgage was a mortgage. You compared rates and that was it. That's no longer the case. Now there are many different types of mortgages. The point here is, once you have found the mortgage lender of your choice, you will more than likely be offered several mortgage options. For example, on a $100,000 thirty-year mortgage:

PLAN A: 9.5% with 3 points to close ($3,000).
PLAN B: 10.0% with 1.5 points to close ($1,500).

A choice like this can be confusing. My experience indicates that Plan B, because of the obvious, more clearly understood savings, would be the option chosen by the majority. That, in most cases, is a mistake.

To determine which plan is best, you must have a formula to establish at what point one plan becomes more profitable than the other. Obviously, Plan B saves you up-front costs of $1,500. The question that needs to be asked, but seldom is, is at what if any point does Plan A's interest-rate savings recover Plan B's up-front savings?

First, ask your banker what the monthly payments are on both amortizations; that is, $100,000 for thirty years at 9.5 percent and at 10.0 percent. The answer is:

PLAN A: Monthly payment = $840.86
PLAN B: Monthly payment = $877.58
_____
Difference $ 36.72

The lower interest rate saves you $36.72 per month. The only remaining calculation is to divide the point savings on Plan B, $1,500, by the monthly savings on Plan A ($1,500 ÷ $36.72). The answer is 40.84. This represents the number of months it will take for the lower interest rate savings to recoup the closing cost savings of the higher mortgage rate. In this example, it will take a little over three years (40.84 months ÷ 12) to recover the savings you would have lost by taking the lower interest rate. From that point on you are going to save money by having opted for Plan A, the plan that to many would have appeared the most expensive.

And what does understanding this math do for the remaining term of your mortgage? The answer is impressive. A thirty-year mortgage runs 360 months. You start saving money after approximately forty-one months. Subtracting that from the amortization means you will save $36.72 for 319 months (360 − 41), which totals $11,713.68 ($36.72 × 319). This saving is a net figure, as you have already, through the first forty-one months, recovered your point-loss differential. The math works on any mortgage option where you are offered a choice between a higher interest rate and lower points or a lower interest rate and higher points. To know which is best for you, the formula must be completed. Only then will you have the information that will allow you to make the best financial decision.

There are instances where the higher rate and lower points would be the best choice. For example, if you are buying a house you know you will have to sell within two years because of a pending transfer, you'll want the up-front savings because there isn't enough time to recover the loss. However, although such circumstances are many and varied, for most of us the lower interest rate offers the best savings. Again, the only way to know that is to do the math.

I feel obligated once again to point out that mortgage options are yet another example of financial institutions making a concerted effort to help the consumer make the wrong choice—in this case on a home, one's biggest investment. Banks have entire departments devoted to packaging and repackaging their services in such a manner as to encourage bad decisions. That's why, on the subject of mortgages, the higher interest rate is associated with the lower closing costs. That's the choice they want you to make. They don't want you to understand the long-term ramifications. They want to be able to advertise to the public and crow to Congress that they offer the consumer financial marketplace competition in the form of wide-ranging options. What they are silent about is how they package the services to confuse, deceive, and lead the consumer to the wrong conclusion.

This example should fortify your resolve to understand more regarding your banking relationships. A tongue-in-cheek rule that contains all too much truth is: If your bank offers you an option that looks appealing, you'd better step back, check your wallet, and grab your calculator before signing any papers.

The Right Term Equals Big Savings

The length of a mortgage has a dramatic impact on its total cost. It's as important as the interest rate, but few homeowners realize how many options they have. And their banker isn't anxious to tell them.

Review in your mind the scenario that took place when you made your mortgage application. After talking to the loan officer, what did you know when your loan was approved? Well, with any luck, you knew the loan's interest rate, the term, the monthly payment amount, and possibly some other sundry, perhaps unimportant things. Let's get to the point. Did you know all of your term options? Term means the length of the amortization, or how many months or years it will take to pay the loan back. Chances are you knew of only one term option, the standard twenty-nine or thirty years. It's no coincidence that the standard length means more money for the bank. But, is it best for you? Compare the following examples of a $100,000 loan at 9 percent, and you'll get an idea of how much money a shorter-loan term can save you.

Example I

Mortgage balance	$100,000.00
Monthly payment (9% for 30 yrs.)	$ 804.63
Total loan repayment	$289,666.80

Example II

Mortgage balance	$100,000.00
Monthly payment (9% for 25 yrs.)	$ 839.20
Total loan repayment	$251,760.00

Example III

Mortgage balance	$100,000.00
Monthly payment (9% for 20 yrs.)	$ 899.73
Total loan repayment	$215,935.20

Example IV

Mortgage balance	$100,000.00
Monthly payment (9% for 15 yrs.)	$ 1,014.27
Total loan repayment	$182,568.60

Example V

Mortgage balance	$100,000.00
Monthly payment (9% for 10 yrs.)	$ 1,266.76
Total repayment	$152,011.20

Unfortunately, most people simply react to the monthly payment the bank quotes them; they determine whether they can afford it, and if so, they accept the loan. They seldom, if ever, go beyond that. What you should do, assuming you can afford the bank's first quote, is ask for all the other term options, as shown above, and then pick the one that has the largest payment you can comfortably afford. As you can see from these examples, the long-term savings can be huge.

Did your banker volunteer all your term possibilities? Did he or she explain the savings? If so, congratulations—you have a banker concerned with your financial welfare. If not—and the odds are you fall into this category—congratulations again, because you've learned firsthand that your bank is not to be trusted. And that is a valuable lesson.

Tax and Insurance Escrow Accounts: R-I-I-I-P

When you open a mortgage account at a bank, your banker more than likely will require that you open an escrow account at the same time. The escrow monies, collected monthly along with your mortgage principal and interest payment, will be set aside to pay your real-estate taxes and homeowners' insurance premiums when they come due.

The banks' reasoning for this requirement—at least the one they will acknowledge—is that an escrow account ensures that all the bills on their collateral are paid on time. When clarifying this aspect of the mortgage to the customer, the banker will explain that it's in the consumer's best interest not to have to worry about these bills. The bank will take care of them, and all you'll have to do is add a "small" amount each and every month to your mortgage payment.

Some banks say nothing at all regarding the escrow requirement and just make it part of the mortgage agreement without knowledgeable consent from the borrower. Others are a little more above board and inform the borrower that it's necessary and required for loan approval.

No matter which approach the bank takes in explaining its escrow requirement, it's either lying or, at best, offering a half-truth.

Financial institutions require escrow accounts for two reasons. The first reason is logical. The second involves profits. First, banks want to ensure that "their" properties are insured against loss ("their" is in quotes because banks see your property as theirs until your final payment is made). The escrow account is their way of insuring their loan investment. They don't want to find out after a disaster that you forgot to pay your insurance bill. That would make their loan collateral useless, which might lead to a loss. Further, they don't want to find out too late that your home is being sold to recoup delinquent taxes, or that the equity is constantly decreasing due to tax liens and accumulated interest liens to the lien holder. If the bank pays your taxes and insurance directly, they know these things cannot happen.

At this juncture it doesn't appear that the bank is taking advantage of anyone, does it? But couldn't a bank achieve the same verifiable results by requiring that the customer produce paid tax and insurance bills when they become due? How they are paid should be of little concern to the bank as long as they are paid. There must be more to this escrow matter. There is.

The fact is, the main reason banks require escrow accounts is because they plan on making large sums of money by investing your escrow balance. They are not satisfied with grossly overpriced closing fees (title expense, appraisal, credit check, and so on) and exorbitant mortgage interest rates; they want still more. That's where your escrow account comes in.

The majority of banking institutions pay little or no interest on their escrow accounts, which means you are making them an interest-free loan every year that mortgage is in existence. The bank loans your escrow monies to other borrowers at a handsome profit, so you can see why they want to have as much to invest as possible. And one of the ways they increase their investable funds is to force mortgage customers to make low- or non-interest-bearing escrow payments.

To show how this works, let's look at a home that has a tax bill of $2,000 and an insurance bill of $450. Your escrow bill is $2,450 over the course of a year, or an additional $204.16 per month. Keeping in mind that a bank generally has the use of half the money collected over a year's time (because the monies are deposited in monthly increments), you have made the bank an interest-free loan of $1,225. Factoring in a conservative loan investment rate of 10 percent, the bank earned $122.50 in interest during the year by using your money while paying you little or nothing. That may not sound exorbitant to you, but it's clearly not fair. Typically the average mortgage runs thirty years, which means at 10 percent the bank will make, in our example, an additional $3,675 over the loan's term. Although that amount may still strike you as being small, the point is that the bank has no legal or moral right to deprive you of this earning asset. That's not a very "friendly" thing to do.

Another aspect of this matter that could cost you money is that the bank anticipates costs, or makes estimates. Sometimes, in order to further protect its position, its overestimates your escrow payments. Even if they do so by only $10 per month, you will have loaned them another $120 per year. If you don't understand your escrow statement (they are designed to be confusing), the overpayment will escalate year after year. At the end of the first year the bank will have an additional $120 to invest for its own gain. At the end of the second they will have $240, and so on. By the time the mortgage has ended they may have had the use of the yearly escrow monies plus another $3,600.

The worst case I have ever seen of this frequent practice was that involving an elderly Illinois couple. Their son was examining their important papers and discovered they had $9,600 in their escrow account. This quite unusual balance was due to over-payments and tax abatements. Their escrow account paid no interest. They had had this balance for almost ten years. With their small present mortgage balance, they could have paid off the loan with the escrow account and still been left with five thousand dollars. No one at their "friendly" bank ever bothered to explain this to the couple. At an average return to the bank of 13 percent over ten years, the bank made $12,480 in interest using the couple's money. The couple, of course, received not one red cent.

The question is, how can we turn a built-in escrow loss such as this into an asset?

The answer is direct and uncomplicated. Tell your bank, before or at your closing, depending on what's appropriate, that you will not agree to an escrow account unless it bears fair, current, market interest rates. Further, the account will be under your name and control. You will pay all the bills as they come due and provide the bank with paid copies. Assuming a fair interest rate, you shouldn't mind keeping the account at that bank. That way the bank can periodically review your balance to ensure that you are making deposits large enough to meet your coming tax and insurance obligations.

Even if the rate of return was as small as 5.5 percent (and you should do much better either at the bank or through another vehicle), over thirty years the return in our example would be $2,021.25. And this doesn't take into account the extra income you could earn through reinvesting the principal and interest. That's not bad for simply knowing what to demand in terms of service.

If your bank will not allow for an interest-bearing escrow account in your name, you may wish to check with the appropriate federal or state banking agency to see if the bank can deny you access to your money. In almost all cases (some states are an exception), the banks' requirement of an escrow account is bank policy, not law. If you find that your bank is breaking the law, you may wish to file a contingency fee class-action law suit, since, if they're doing it to you, they're doing it to others.

Lastly, I believe that, regardless of the law in your state, if your bank is that greedy with your money, you should find another bank.

You Can Pay Your Bank $289,666.80 for Your $100,000 Home, or You Can Buy It for "Free"

Is it really possible to buy a home for free? Amazingly, yes. It should be obvious that to accomplish this important financial goal you have to deviate from traditional thinking.

For most of us, the one time when we are more or less forced to deal with our bank is when we buy a home. Not many can afford to pay cash, which means you are looking at a long-term mortgage loan commitment. Before discussing the mortgage and its amortization, you need a basic understanding of how a mortgage works. Mortgages are usually the largest debt your family will incur, and that fact alone should get your attention. Unfortunately, most people never understand what a home actually costs. If they paid $100,000 for the house, they think that was their cost. Wrong. The cost of the house is what you pay in total, and that includes your mortgage repayment.

When the bank offers a loan rate and quotes the monthly payment, the family simply decides whether or not they can afford that expense. If the answer is yes, they go ahead. Very seldom do they calculate the total to be repaid. The financial institution would rather that you never do.

It is a general rule in today's market that for every dollar of mortgage money you borrow, you will pay back—depending on the interest rate—two to four dollars. Consequently, if you borrow $100,000, you are going to pay back $200,000 to $400,000. More than likely, when you signed your mortgage agreement the lender never made that information obvious. Typically, the bank's mortgage documentation will tell you what your monthly payment is, when it's due, the annual percentage rate (APR), the closing costs, the loan's term, and so on, but it seldom makes it easy for you to determine how much you will ultimately repay. If they did, many customers would demand a better deal (rate), as they would understand the true nature of the debt. Borrowing $100,000 is one thing; owing $200,000 to $400,000 is another. Look at your house. Is it really worth that much?

Determining your total mortgage obligation is easy: Multiply your monthly payment by twelve (months in the year). Multiply that sum by your loan's term, for example, twenty-nine or thirty years.

Clearly, when you are talking about a debt as large as your mortgage, it behooves you to try to lower your interest rate, but that's another subject, rate negotiation, and we've already covered that. I simply want once again to make you aware of the important concept that loan rates are negotiable. An aggressive loan customer can take advantage of this little-known fact. Calculate how much money you will borrow in your lifetime, and factor in even a small, one-percentage-point reduction in costs. You will be stunned at the savings that can be realized. You must be willing to negotiate and haggle in order to retain as much of your earnings as possible. I estimate that through simple rate negotiations you can, at a minimum, save as much as fifty thousand dollars over the course of your financial lifetime. And that figure doesn't take into account the additional money you could make by investing those savings.

Never forget, any loan interest-rate reduction is worth fighting for. Don't settle for less than a fair deal. Remember, banks make good loan customers like you pay more than they should so they can offset their losses with their bad-loan customers. You can't afford to pay for the bank's lending mistakes.

Note: From this point forward, we are going to use as an example a mortgage loan of $100,000 at 9 percent for thirty years. The loan has monthly payments of $804.63 for a total repayment cost of $289,666.80.

The first thing you must realize is that if you follow the bank's loan amortization schedule (monthly payment timetable) there is nothing I or anyone else can do to reduce the true net cost of your home. The reason becomes obvious when you recognize that mortgage payments are recalculated every month on a declining balance. This means it will be many years before you even start denting the principal. For example, in our sample loan the first payment is broken down as follows:

Total monthly payment.........................$804.63
Interest.......................................$750.00
Principal reduction............................$ 54.63

The first month's principal reduction is only 6.8 percent of the payment itself. You can see how, with this schedule, you will be paying the bank back virtually forever, which is exactly what the bank wants.

How do we turn this around? The answer is to add an additional principal payment with each monthly payment. For our example, we will use an added fifty dollars per month (a conservative figure—you can probably do better). When you make an added monthly payment, the entire amount is subtracted from the loan's principal. Interesting, when we make the bank's first scheduled payment of $804.63, your loan is reduced by only $54.63, but when you add just $50.00 more you almost double the reduction.

What effect does this have on your loan? The startling answer in this example is that by making this small additional payment you will repay your thirty-year loan in just 23.4 years. You reduced your obligation by six-plus years, or $63,565.77 ($804.63 × 79 months). And all it cost you was $14,050 ($50.00 × 281 months). Let's look at our savings so far.

Payments to bank.........................$226,101.03
$50 additional payments ....$ 14,050.00
Total $240,151.03

Granted, that's still a lot of money, but we have gone a long way toward recovering your scheduled mortgage payments. Look at the savings:

Bank amortization cost......................$289,666.80
New total cost............................$240,151.03
Total savings ....$ 49,515.77

This should make clear that you should never accept the bank's way of doing business. It's just too costly. You must use nontraditional alternatives.

We have now made substantial progress, but we haven't reached our goal of completely recovering the mortgage expense—making it "free." The accelerated loan repayment was just the first step in our system. As it stands, we have saved 17 percent of what the example loan would have cost.

The next step is using the saving of time accumulated by the first step. If you were originally willing to pay the bank the last six-plus years of the mortgage, you should be willing to pay yourself instead. In this case, you would continue to make your monthly payments of $804.63, but they would be made to your own saving or investment program. What would your accumulated investment be worth with payments of $804.63 invested in a plan that returned 10 percent (you should be able to average this rate or better) over the last six-plus years of what is now your paid-off mortgage? The answer is an amazing $89,440.26.

Of course, if you make these payments to yourself, you still have an expenditure and that must be recalculated into your net cost. That is to say, the comparison must again be with the amount you actually paid. It doesn't matter who got the money. Let's review where we are:

Paid by customer
    to bank and self $289,666.80
Balance of savings
    plan after 6-plus years.................$ 89,440.26
Unrecovered mortgage expense.............$200,226.54

We aren't doing too badly. By ignoring the bank's amortization schedule and adding as little as $50.00 per month to your payment, you saved $49,515.77, or six-plus years' worth of expense minus the added monthly payments. Then, by using the time savings to your advantage and making what was a liability into an asset, your savings jumped to a whopping $89,440.26. We have now saved 30.9 percent of the real cost of your home.

The next and final step actually must be the first step you take in order to recover the entire cost of your scheduled mortgage payments. It's imperative when you buy a home that you dissect the entire transaction. That is the total mortgage repayment, the added payments you will make, and what the savings balance will be at the end of the thirty years. You should have this information available for your own education and, more important, to determine the final piece of the puzzle. In our example, you would still have an unrecovered mortgage expense of $200,226.54. To recoup that amount, you are going to buy a Grade A Municipal Bond from a local security house. This purchase must be made at the time you sign your mortgage, as it should have the same term as your mortgage. In our example, we are using an interest rate of 8.5 percent to buy the bond. This rate changes daily, and could be higher or lower, but that won't adversely affect the end result of the investment. In this case, the bond would cost $17,019.25 ($200,226.54 × .085); you should refactor this into your equation so that the cost of the bond is recovered. At the end of thirty years, you will receive $200,226.54 in cash, and all of it will be free from federal income taxes. It is assumed here that you can afford to pay cash for the bond, and if that's the case, you are finished.

Those who might not be able to afford the bond purchase can borrow additional money in their mortgage—enough to buy the bond. Of course, the added amount will have to be recalculated into your program, but it won't change the bottom line, which is this: At the end of the term of your loan, you will have your home free and clear and all of your scheduled mortgage payments in the bank in your name.

This system is, by necessity, flexible. There are many variables to consider. For example: You may wish to borrow money for the bond on a short-term note of your own choosing, as opposed to adding its cost to your mortgage. Maybe you can make additional monthly payments of as much as two hundred dollars off and on. Perhaps your savings plan returns as little as 8 percent, or maybe as much as 13 percent. There are no parameters to the system, which is to your advantage. Notwithstanding particulars, one thing cannot be denied—you are going to pay either your mortgage holder or yourself. The choice seems obvious. The bank's way, at the end of thirty years, you will have your home free and clear. My way, you'll have your home free and clear, and, using this example, a savings plan and municipal bond totaling $289,666.80. And the beauty is, it didn't cost you a penny more than you were willing to pay for the house alone.

One final thought. Has your banker ever explained this principle to you, or one like it? If they're really that "friendly," if they really care about you and your family, why not?

There's More Than One Way to Skin the Cat

We just reviewed the real cost of a home mortgage and how it can be substantially reduced and/or negated entirely. There is one additional technique that you should be aware of, as it offers you a great deal of flexibility in the treatment of your mortgage.

Remember from the previous discussion that our objective is to cut the term by approximately one-third so we may apply the other savings and investment aspects of our reduction plan. This can also be accomplished without added monthly principal payments. How? By greatly accelerating your term in a most unusual manner.

Accelerating the term offers the same result as adding additional monthly principal payments. You accelerate your term by remitting a portion of your payment in advance. Let's again use an example loan of $100,000 at 9 percent for thirty years, with monthly payments of $804.63 and a total mortgage repayment after thirty years of $289,666.80.

We are going to make it easy to diagram and understand the acceleration technique by using a two-week payment cycle. Instead of making our payment monthly, we are going to make one-half of our payment every two weeks. In this example, instead of making monthly payments of $804.63, we are going to make semimonthly payments of $402.32. What does this accomplish?

As hard as it is to believe, it reduces your mortgage term by more than six years. In real dollars, that means a savings of $60,347.25 ($804.63 × 75 months). Now, add our investment principal with the savings realized and you have a formula for sizable financial success.

This reduction works because of two factors. First, since your mortgage will be an amortized simple-interest note, you are charged the interest rate multiplied by the present outstanding balance, multiplied by the term between payments—as opposed to an installment loan, where you are constantly charged the interest multiplied by the original balance. Obviously, the more quickly you make payments, the less interest you owe. And the less interest you owe, the more of your payment can be applied to principal. And the more quickly you reduce the principal, the sooner the loan will be paid.

There is another important aspect to this plan: You are forcing yourself to make additional payments, although you may not have realized it, because there is an imbalance between the payment dates you will use and those on the calendar. In other words, twenty-six biweekly payments is equal to thirteen monthly payments. The obvious reason for this is that months aren't exactly four weeks long, so your biweekly schedule accelerates your term by one month a year. This added payment aids in the reduction in interest due to your biweekly prepayments.

Now for those of you who don't believe you can afford the extra month's expense, I say that some reduction is better than none. If you wish, you may take your yearly expense—in our example, $9,655.56 ($804.63 × 12 months)—divide it by twenty-four, and make that payment of $402.32 at the halfway point of each month. Or, you can take that amount and divide it by fifty-two and make weekly payments of $185.68. In both instances your payments, in total dollars, will be the same as what you would have paid anyway, but you will still save thousands. Here's how it works: Using the weekly payment schedule, your first weekly payment will save approximately three weeks' interest on the principal reduction amount, the second payment two weeks', and the third week one week's interest. This occurs every month. And that interest savings will be applied to your mortgage principal, which reduces your term obligation.

Of course, it's easier and more profitable to use the biweekly payment plan, but if that's not feasible it's important to create savings with what you can afford. To reiterate, even if you don't raise your monthly expense one dollar, there is still money to be saved by accelerating your term.

Because of the impact a mortgage has on most of our finances, it's logical to make every attempt to control and use that investment. That's why I have reviewed these various options.

Any one of these techniques can help you. The principle discussed in this section can be combined and used in conjunction with the other techniques previously outlined. Or, maybe one year you can use the biweekly payment plan, while later on you can add additional principle payments as your income increases. Don't forget, under most market conditions, for every dollar you borrow you are going to pay back two to four. The reverse is also true. For every dollar you save you are saving two to four. So don't think a monthly savings of five, ten, twenty, or fifty dollars isn't much, because what you're really talking about may be twenty, forty, eighty, and two hundred dollars.

How to Improve Your Mortgage

Obtaining the best possible mortgage when you buy a home is not the end of the mortgage equation. You should always try to improve your position. This brings us to your remortgage option.

We live in a time of financial volatility, meaning interest rates fluctuate often and severely, so it makes sense to review your mortgage as it compares with today's rates. This is one of the reasons I recommend a fixed-rate mortgage, because when interest rates go up, you aren't affected. When they go down, you have the option of remortgaging and lowering your expense. You have the best of both worlds when you retain control of your mortgage via a fixed rate.

Unfortunately, knowing when it's profitable to remortgage is not as obvious as you might like. If you're reapplying with your present mortgage holder, you'll find that banks are applying substantial remortgaging fees to discourage customers from trying to improve their loan. For those who do remortgage, the bank wants to make enough in fees to offset the "loss" they experience in lowering your mortgage rate (i.e., the bank will earn less monthly interest). If you're remortgaging with a new institution, you will still be faced with closing and other costs and in many cases those costs will be exorbitant. In either case, you have to understand how to determine if remortgaging makes sense, and that entails more than just realizing a rate reduction. You have to ensure that the rate reduction will pay for itself after you pay the expenses of acquiring the lower rate.

As a rule, start thinking about remortgaging when rates have fallen, at a minimum, one full percentage point below your current mortgage rate. When rates fall that amount or more, go to the bank and ask for your mortgage payoff balance. Then ask what your new monthly payment would be if you renegotiated your mortgage at the new lower interest rate (remember to shop for a lower rate at three or more institutions, or use a mortgage alternative). For comparison, have them add your remortgaging and closing costs to your payoff balance before giving you your new monthly payment figure. Now subtract your new monthly payment from your old monthly payment. This is your monthly savings. Then divide your remortgaging and closing costs by the savings figure. This gives you the number of months it will take to recoup your expenses. From that point forward you will start realizing an actual savings. With this knowledge, whether or not remortgaging makes sense becomes evident. Either it pays or it doesn't. For example, if you determine that it will take three years to recover your costs and you're planning on moving in two years, remortgaging is not a viable option.

Let's look at an example. Your present $100,000 thirty-year mortgage has a balance of $94,059.81. You have twenty-two years remaining at 10.5 percent. The bank will remortgage at 9 percent with closing costs and remortgaging fees of $2,400. How long will it take before you start saving money?

Mortgage balance $94,059.81
Remortgaing and closing costs 2,400.00
Total 96,459.81
Present mortgage payment 914.75
New mortgage payment
($96,459.81 at 9% with a 22-year
    amortization 840.33
Difference 74.42

The $2,400 (remortgaging and closing costs) divided by $74.42 (the difference between your old mortgage payment and your new mortgage payment) comes to 32.2 months. That's how long it will take you to break even on the transaction. That means the last 231.8 months of your mortgage will bring you a profit of $74.42 per month for a total savings of $17,250.55.

Improving your mortgage is not something your bank wants you to do—which should tell you how important it is for you to do just that.

BANK CREDIT CARDS

Bank Credit Cards—Bad for You, Good for the Bank

If interest rates were relatively low, what would you do if your mortgage was approved, but at 19 percent? Or your car loan at 22 percent? In both examples you would immediately withdraw your application and move all your banking business to another institution. You would not allow your finances to be assaulted in such a manner.

And yet, through the miracle of questionable packaging, much of the daily borrowing in this country is accomplished at exceptionally high rates that completely ignore the influence of the market. Banks realized years ago that their noncompetitive hold on interest rates could be further enhanced if they could hide the true cost of money from the borrower. Hence was born plastic money, or credit cards.

A sobering fact: Affluent people did not get that way by paying more for things than necessary. That's why you should never borrow for depreciating, nonessential assets. It follows, then, that although they may use a credit card for convenience, affluent people never let interest charges accrue, as that would be adding to the real cost of the purchase. The only people who borrow using credit cards are people who either do not understand the system, or have no other method to purchase the use of funds.

Clearly, even at a superficial look, it should be obvious that using a credit card is dangerous. That is why banks have spent millions in advertising, marketing, and promotion to obliterate the true cost of using their credit cards. That is why most people cannot tell you the interest rate on their card charges and/or what method of interest computation is used by the bank issuing the card. As sad as that is, it's true. Banks have been most successful at hiding important facts from the credit-card consumer. For example, you will often see or receive offers for credit cards with no apparent mention of its interest rate or an exceptionally low "Introductory Rate." If your application is subsequently approved, you will receive a notice of rate along with reams of other materials, but at this point, after the passage of a number of weeks, most people don't bother reading all the fine print, or they just don't understand it. In addition, hardly anyone understands how the interest is calculated.

In any market, banks cannot justify by cost analysis their exorbitant interest rates on credit cards. The proof lies in recent history. A number of years ago, home mortgage rates were at 16 percent. The prime rate was at 20 percent, consumer loans were at 18 percent, commercial loans at prime plus 3 percent to 4 percent, and credit cards at 18 percent to 22 percent. A few years later, mortgages dropped below 8 percent. Prime was at 7 percent, consumer loans were reduced to 9 percent or below, and commercial loans were at straight prime. All rates dropped almost in half, yet credit cards were still charging 18 percent to 22 percent interest.

The question is, why didn't credit-card rates drop, too? The answer is simple. Banks don't have to get into rate competition with their credit cards because the consumer doesn't know what the rates really are in the first place. Also, only people who can afford it the least use credit cards for anything other than convenience, so banks know they have a captive, probably financially uneducated, market. Because of that, they don't fear financial retribution (that is, loss of accounts). Can you imagine a bank telling General Motors, at a time when prime is 7 percent, that they have to pay 22 percent to borrow money? GM would take its business elsewhere. Unfortunately, credit-card users aren't so discerning. That perpetuates their high cost of money, which subsequently helps keep them among the less affluent. It is a vicious cycle, in large part orchestrated by the banking community.

Not only are most people unaware of their credit-card interest rate, but the system is designed to further muddle the situation until the consumer completely forgets he is entering into a financial lending transaction. If every time you wanted to borrow money using your credit card you had to go into the bank and sign a separate loan agreement indicating an interest rate of 19 percent or more, you might rethink the purchase. But, with a card, it's easy to forget the real issue, which is this: Regardless of what you are purchasing, you are in the process of borrowing money. How much it will cost you depends on the card's interest rate and the bank's method of interest computation, and whether or not the card starts accruing interest immediately when used. Regardless, the cost will be plenty.

I hope by using the following example-quiz I can convince you never to use that credit card for a loan again, except possibly in an emergency.

Let's assume a mythical family with a credit-card debt of $2,000 (below average for many families), additional monthly purchases of only $20 and a minimum repayment of $45 per month at 22 percent. The question is, how long will it take this family to pay off their credit card debt?

The answer? The debt will never be paid.

With the minimum payment of $45, only $8.33 is principal (the interest is $36.67 per month). The principal reduction will be offset by the additional monthly purchases. Financially this family will be constantly going backwards.

How costly is this method of borrowing over the course of one's life? To nail the point, let's assume this couple is twenty-five years old when they acquire this credit-card debt balance. At the age of sixty-five, they will have paid back $21,600, and they will still owe a balance of more than $2,000. In effect, they will not have reduced their original debt at all. Forty years of payments, and they still owe the same monies as when they started. We are talking economic self-destruction here. This should make it clear that banks package their credit cards in such a way as to rape the financial future of many unfortunate families. You can't let this happen to you.

If you have to borrow, it should be obvious that you could do so at a substantially reduced rate, as many credit-cards have an interest rate of 18 to 22 percent, which leaves a great deal of room for expense reduction. Almost any personal loan would save you considerable money. At any rate, borrowing using the standard bank credit card is not a viable alternative.

Now, before you say that you don't really borrow using "plastic," I have to ask, Have you ever been assessed an interest charge on your card? Remember, many cards now charge from the moment you use the card, which means you will automatically accrue interest charges even if you pay the entire balance each month when you receive the bill. If that's the case, you borrowed using plastic. Others who don't pay off their entire bill obviously borrow using plastic.

Remember, just because you bought a new suit as opposed to receiving cash in hand, you still borrowed money.

Sadly, many will have credit-card debt for the rest of their lives. It is truly a bank-designed financial treadmill. I have to ask why would you allow yourself and your family to be abused in this manner? This is a prime example of paying more for something than necessary. If you have to borrow money, that's fine. But if you use the standard bank credit card to accomplish that goal, you are making a financial mistake that rates a ten on the one-to-ten mistake meter. (To find a low-rate bank credit card, call Bankcardholders of America at 1-(540) 389-5445. For four dollars they can provide an up-to-date listing of preferred credit cards with low interest rates, and those that have no annual fee.)

Above, we discussed the credit-card treadmill, and how the issuing companies and banks have designed the system to ensure their maximum return, neverending consumer debt, and confusion in creditese, which allows for taking the most from those who can afford it the least. Most bank credit cards have made consumer abuse an art form, and they have done so not by providing a legitimate consumer service, but by exploiting a segment of the financial market. They then expand the abuse further by misdirecting that market segment. A good example of this deliberate confusion is the variable-rate credit card.

When one bank credit-card company announced to its members that it was offering a variable interest rate on its cards, it sent out certificates providing the option of changing from the fixed rate. New members were offered both options (that is, fixed or variable rate). The variable interest rate was "at the prime rate, as published in the *Wall Street Journal*, plus 9.4 percent." The change, should you opt for the variable rate, would not be reversible (that is, once your fixed rate is gone, it's gone for good).

Before going into specifics, let me quote you some of the premises in the ad. You decide if this bank is being fair.

"Interest rates have been making front-page news quite regularly these past few months. And, at [name of bank], we're committed to helping our valued Cardmembers take advantage of favorable rates."

"This variable rate could save you a significant amount of money."

Of course, the ad forgot to mention that there is another side to the coin. What happens if prime goes up? You guessed it: Your savings will be history, and you will be locked in to a roller-coaster ride on the Interest Rate Express. Historically, we know how high prime can go, and with this variable-interest-rate credit card, there is no cap on the upside.

Also, the ad copy gave examples only of savings. There was no balance to the presentation. Last, the bank knew exactly what it was doing (that is, setting up the financially uneducated cardholders for added expense), or it wouldn't have instituted the nonreversal clause that prohibits going back to the fixed rate.

As of this writing, most bank credit cards offer the variable-rate option. More will follow.

If you remembered my comments on the adjustable-rate mortgage, you knew up front what my reaction to the variable-rate credit card was going to be. Well, you were right, but let's go further. The card is a much worse deal than the variable-rate mortgage (certainly not in volume and exposure, but in principle), for as discussed earlier, credit-card borrowing is financially destructive on its face. This new credit-card twist is a disgrace. No one in his right mind would opt for this method of interest computation, and the company knows that. This leaves us with the sad, but not surprising, conclusion that banks are making every possible attempt to take as much from their less-fortunate customers as possible—again, under very relaxed consumer-protection laws.

You have been warned. Do not accept a variable-rate credit card. You will save money following that advice.

Of course, if you really want to save, don't borrow using plastic. At the very least, get a low, fixed-rate card that has no annual fee and charges no interest if you pay your balance in full.

The subject of bank credit cards is another example of the banking industry's propensity to gouge the financial consumer whenever possible.

Here's one more case in point: credit-card insurance. Credit-card customers are constantly being bombarded with ads for insurance on their credit cards. The ads are very scary, giving the impression that it can save you a bundle if there's a problem with lost or stolen cards. Unfortunately, it's all a lie. The law states that you are exposed to a maximum responsibility, of only fifty dollars for each card that's lost or stolen. If you report the card lost or stolen immediately, before it's used illegally, your exposure is zero. Next time you see an ad for credit-card insurance, read it with this knowledge in mind and see if you don't agree: The bank is trying to rip you off. The fact is, credit card insurance, for most people, is a waste of money, because you're paying for something you're almost entirely entitled to for free.

OTHER BANK "SERVICES"

Checking Accounts

I don't recommend having a bank checking account. There are too many better, cheaper alternatives (see Appendix, "Banking Alternatives").

Then too, if you have an interest-bearing checking account at your bank, the rate you're receiving is seldom competitive.

Over and above that, you have the problem of how banks treat your deposits. Prior to the 1988 Epedited Funds Availability Act (EFAA), banks arbitrarily dictated hold periods for your deposits. In many banks even cash deposits were subject to a hold (waiting period) before the depositor could use the funds. Imagine that! The reason banks had such ludicrous hold policies was, of course, profits. The longer they could hold on to your money, the more money they could make with it. Hold policies had nothing to do with protecting the bank against checks returned against your account (the excuse used by most banks); they were solely for profits. Again, some banks even put a hold on cash! In addition to allowing the bank to use your money longer free of charge, these outrageous policies often created an expensive overdraft or uncollected-funds charge against your account when, in fact, no overdraft or uncollected-fund situation existed. Again, more bank profit.

The abuse was so blatant that Congress passed the EFAA against the will of the banking industry, something that seldom happens. Of course, bankers didn't take kindly to the Act even though Congress wrote it in such a manner that it sounds much better than it is. In fact, for some banks, the Act gave them cover of law to extend their hold policy, not reduce it.

The cause of this problem is that the EFAA stipulations refer to banking or business days rather than calendar days, which was the criterion used previously. So what appears to be fewer days required for funds to clear often *adds* days to the hold process. Congress, as I've said, so often does the bankers' bidding even if it has to do so surreptitiously.

The Act also gives a bank many exceptions to its mandated funds-collection schedule. Here are five of the legal rationales for potential delays in allowing you access to your money. I hope you're sitting down.

1. You deposit checks in excess of five thousand dollars in any one day.

2. You redeposit a check that has been returned unpaid.

3. You have repeatedly overdrawn your account in the last six months ("repeatedly" is not defined).

4. There is an emergency, such as a bank equipment failure. (Why should this be your problem—will the bank give you credit for a deposit you couldn't make because your car broke down?)

5. The bank believes a check you deposit will not be paid (this has to qualify as the quintessential catchall).

There are additional exceptions for new accounts. Exceptions to the hold schedule can be as long as eight business days. Taking into account nonbusiness days, the actual hold could be as long as twelve calendar days. All this waiting, despite that virtually all checks clear within the first forty-eight hours.

There is more bad news. Many banks, for a variety of reasons, have a cutoff time for deposits. Usually it's in the early afternoon. If you make a deposit after that time, your deposit goes into the next day's business, which adds a full day to your hold time. If you have checks that clear on that extra day, too bad. Although you may have deposited thousands of dollars in excess of what was needed to pay those checks, because of the deposit-cutoff anomaly you may be assessed an overdraft charge. And that brings us to the subject of overdrafts. I want to discuss them because they are a perfect example of how unconscienable bank fees are.

If you overdraft your checking account you've committed a misdemeanor under the Deceptive Practices Act. Strictly interpreted, even if you cover the check before it clears, at the time you wrote the check, you still broke the law. Obviously, this strict legal interpretation is seldom enforced against the average consumer. If it was, half the country would be in jail. But enforcement of the law is not the point. I highly recommend that you never purposely overdraft your account. Not because it's against the law, but rather because it's a shoddy way to do business.

I am ignoring, of course, those who overdraft their account for the purpose of fraud. That is a criminal act and criminals should be prosecuted.

For most people, however, overdrafting an account is usually an honest error. Maybe you made a mistake in balancing your checkbook. Maybe you arrived late at the bank with your deposit. There are many legitimate ways an overdraft can happen, but that is not the issue. Then too, as discussed above, perhaps the bank's hold policies created an overdraft on your account.

In fairness to the bank, when you overdraft your account you do cause extra work for the bank staff, and an obvious extra bank expense. The bank has a right to be compensated even if your overdraft was accidental. That's not arguable.

How much does the bank spend processing an overdraft (OD)? Most bank cost-analysis surveys indicate a cost of about a dollar.

Computer cost per OD	$0.25
Employee's processing cost	0.50
Mailing cost of OD notice	0.32
Total	$1.07

An overdraft charge can be as high as twenty-five dollars per check. That means those banks that charge such fees are making a percentage return on their "investment" (actual overdraft-processing cost) of almost 2,400 percent. That seems a little high to me, especially in light of what little interest they pay on our savings accounts.

As unreasonable as it is, numerous banks are charging twenty-five dollars per check. That means if you have three checks bounce on the same day, you are charged seventy-five dollars. Although they incur no additional expense for multiple-check ODs on the same day, some banks charge for each check! Their returns become astronomical.

Although bankers would like us to think of OD fees as their protection against returned-check losses, in fact ODs are one of banks' major income-producers. That should give you an indication of their true intentions in assessing unreasonable, unjustifiable fees for sending our checks back through the clearing system. Those fees are not for the purpose of discouraging customer OD abuse. They are for generating huge bank profits—profits that make the return on the most profitable loan in the bank's loan portfolio pale by comparison. Banks, contrary to their rhetoric, want you to overdraft your account—and the more frequently, the better. Unless they decide to pay the overdraft, which in most instances is highly unlikely, the bank has no exposure to loss. Therefore, each overdraft becomes almost pure profit.

Overdrafting your account is wrong if done intentionally, and even if you made an honest mistake you should be assessed a fair fee for the extra work you caused. But overdraft fees charged by most banks cannot be justified by cost analysis. Furthermore, a percentage of ODs and uncollected-funds charges are created by the bank. We should never have to pay a fee under those circumstances.

One last observation: Charges and fees on bank checking accounts have skyrocketed lately. So much so, it's hard to keep up with them. The rise in fees would be bad enough, but now we have to contend with being charged for things we never were charged for before. For example, some banks now have a charge, usually three dollars, for calling to request your account balance. Yet another reason to use an alternative.

How does all this square with the "friendly bank" image your bank advertises?

How does this square with my theory that your bank is an enemy?

Overdraft Checking—A Bad Way to Borrow Money

Overdraft checking allows you to write checks for more than you have in your account without the fear that your check will be returned. At most banks, the overdraft-checking interest rate, although it varies from bank to bank, is higher than most consumer loan vehicles, but lower than that of most credit cards.

At face value, overdraft checking doesn't sound too bad. It protects you from the embarrassment of an overdraft return, the expense of an overdraft, and the usually high cost of most bank lending. Unfortunately, you have to delve deeper to determine the true cost/benefit ratio of the service.

Most overdraft checking plans work in one of two ways, or a combination of both. In the first case, the bank will deposit an amount rounded to the next hundred dollars required to cover your overdraft. For example, if you overdraft your account by $105, the bank will deposit $200 in that account. Naturally, you're charged interest on the higher amount—in this case $200, even though only $95 of the loan ($200 − $105) will remain in your checking account. Until you write a check against the difference, the bank will be using the $95 for its own investment purposes, notwithstanding the fact that you're paying interest on it.

Let's say this bank charges 12 percent (many banks charge more) on its overdraft-protection accounts. That's 1 percent per month, which is certainly less expensive than a bank credit card, which may run as high as 19 percent or 20 percent. But are you really paying 12 percent on the amount you actually needed to borrow? No, of course not. Your monthly cost for the two hundred dollars is two dollars at 12 percent. Remember, you only needed to borrow $105. The two dollars bank charge is equal to a 22.8 percent charge on that amount ($2 ÷ $105 × 12). You see, by depositing money you don't need, the bank almost doubles your expense. As is so often the case, when you deal with banks you have to understand the entire transaction, even unstated nuances, before you can determine your net cost. The bank hopes you never do that, because then you would reject many bank services as unnecessary and overpriced.

The other usual overdraft checking method used is that the bank pays the amount of the overdraft and charges an interest rate on that amount—let's use 12 percent again—but in addition assesses a transaction fee for each overdraft check that causes a loan to be made to your account. Here too the fees vary. Suppose the bank has a one dollar fee for each check. What effect does that have on your actual cost? Staying with our example of a $105 overdraft, your interest rate cost for the month will be $1.05. But to that we have to add $1.00, so your total charge is $2.05, or an equivalent interest rate of 23.4 percent ($2.05 ÷ $105.00 × 12). It should be noted that a per-check fee will have less of an interest-rate impact the more money you borrow; however, the majority of such transactions involve smaller amounts. Regardless of the actual interest rate per transaction, you will be paying more than what you thought you would be charged—which is, of course, what the bank had in mind all along.

Now let's combine the two approaches and see how ridiculously costly this can become. Again, you overdraft your account by $105. The bank deposits two hundred dollars, and assesses a one dollar per-check transaction fee. The stated interest rate (APR) on your loan agreement is 12 percent. In this case, your actual interest charge for the month is two dollars. To that we have to add the one-dollar transaction fee, for a total of three dollars. A three-dollar monthly charge for a loan of $105 is equal to an interest-rate expense of 34.3 percent ($3 ÷ $105 × 12), or almost triple the rate the bank is advertising.

All of a sudden this service doesn't sound so appealing, does it? That's because it's not. Certainly there are instances where one would want such protection, and, as with credit cards, if you're going to use the service, do so for convenience only. Don't actually borrow money using your overdraft-protection account. The bank would like you to do just that, as they know their net return is far in excess of their stated APR. This inexpensive-looking method of borrowing, as I've shown above, isn't inexpensive at all. That's why banks would like you to rollover your loan month after month. To that end, many banks will even debit your checking account for your minimum payment amount so you won't have to be "bothered" paying the bill. That sounds good, but the bank has ulterior motives. Since its bill-paying service, in this instance, pays only the minimum required, it ensures that you will have a loan balance next month whether you make additional purchases of money or not. And next month that same balance will be subject to another interest charge. The bank would rather you never pay off the balance, which is also its philosophy regarding credit-card balances. The bank wants you to borrow as much as it believes you can conceivably pay back, and then keep paying on that debt forever. You can't afford to be victim of this dubious marketing technique. A revolving line of overdraft protection should never become a permanent debt.

Overdraft checking sounds like a bargain. It's not. It is, in many cases, nothing more than an expensive way to go more deeply into debt. My principal objection is not the concept, but rather how banks market and practice the service. It appears to be one thing when it's actually something quite different. Anytime you enter into a lending transaction that may cost you three times what you thought it would, you've got a problem.

When you remember that many of the overdrafts the bank will be protecting you from are caused by its own unreasonable hold policy on your deposits, the misrepresentation and hidden cost of this service become even more objectionable.

If you're not going to take my advice and use an alternative to a bank checking account, but want to protect your account from an overdraft, ask your banker to "red flag" your account. This means when your account becomes overdrawn the bank will call and you'll have until the end of that day to make a deposit to cover the overdrafted amount. In effect, you'll have overdraft protection at no charge. If your bank refuses your request, it's time to move your account(s).

It Doesn't Pay to Save at a Bank Anymore

As with my reservations about bank checking accounts, I don't know why anyone would save at a bank. Here also, there are too many better alternatives (see Appendix, "Banking Alternatives"). Bank savings rates are almost always substantially below the market—so much so that saving at a bank can often prove a net loss once you factor in your taxes and inflation. Why save at an institution that pays so little interest? Why have your individual retirement account (IRA) at a bank when you could be earning more? It makes no sense.

To some people, FDIC insurance is the key. They want that safety factor. We've already discussed the FDIC, so I won't elaborate again. But remember, FDIC insurance is more illusory than real (this is especially true when reviewing a bank's IRA options; in any case only one hundred thousand dollars of its grandiose account projections will be insured). Also, when's the last time a major brokerage house, as opposed to a bank, went under? What about Discover, Household Financial Services, Beneficial Finance? The fact is, each of these savings alternatives, as well as others, has a corporate financial statement that is stronger than that of most banks', and offers a form of insurance that may be better than the FDIC. And all pay better interest.

There is another, new reason not to save at a bank, in addition to their low rates and substantial penalties for early withdrawal. Many banks are now charging fees against savings accounts. One such fee is a dormant-account fee. A dormant account is a bank account that has had no activity over a certain period of time. Under normal circumstances that would be all one could say about the subject. However, with deregulation of the financial industry, the rules have changed.

First, as regards your savings account, the bank is required to act as an agent of the state. This has always been the case, and it is not the bank's fault. Individual state laws dictate that financial institutions purge their account files each year, and those accounts that have had no activity (interest posting does not qualify as activity), must be turned over to the state. In some states the dormant time criterion is five years, in others seven.

This presents a problem for many financial consumers. For instance, the elderly who may have forgotten an account they have had for decades. Estates have problems, too, as the deceased may have been the only person who knew where an account was located. Parents sometimes open an account for their children only to forget it as time passes. There are any number of ways an account becomes dormant and then becomes state property. These accounts amount to millions of dollars each year.

I believe that since a bank account is fiduciary in nature, it should be forced by law to ensure the customer is notified his or her account has become dormant, and the account monies returned to the owner, as opposed to remitting to the state. However, as this represents substantial state income, most states are more concerned with securing their cut than in doing what is right.

Nevertheless, should you realize that you have an account that has not been used in years, and the bank says it turned the funds over to the state, you can recoup your money. Petition the agency that received the funds (the bank will give you the name and address) and, provided you can prove ownership (your passbook or a copy of your Social Security card usually is adequate), it will give your money back. This takes time, and the agency will only remit what the bank sent them. They will not, under most state guidelines, pay you any interest even if they have had your money for ten or twenty years.

More important to this discussion is the bank's role since deregulation. Since then, many of the laws that were designed to protect the consumer, however inadequately, have disappeared. In the case of a dormant account, this now means the bank is allowed to take some or all the money from an account long before it has to remit it to the state.

How? Numerous banks are now assessing exorbitant service charges on all accounts that have no monthly activity. Each month the account balance is decreased by a service fee of X dollars. In most cases, dormant accounts are no longer paid interest regardless of the balance amount, and the bank's profit center starts eating away at the principal. This policy is enacted on both savings and checking accounts.

Such finagling is just one more reason our country ranks last in individual savings rates among industrialized nations. The way the banks are doing business, it doesn't pay to save.

Banks are no longer satisfied with underpaying our savings interest—they want whatever principal they can get, too. The sad fact is that since most dormant accounts are relatively small and very seldom remembered by the rightful owner, the bank and the state—if anything is left after the bank utilizes it—will bleed the balance dry.

Protect yourself and your estate. If you have accounts, keep them active by making a small deposit or withdrawal periodically, preferably monthly if possible. Check with your financial institution on which account service charges it levies, and how much. If they are excessive, move to another bank. Also, make a list of all your accounts and where they are located. Keep the list where your family can find it at all times.

You worked hard for the money in your bank accounts, and it belongs to you. Protect it. If you don't, many banks will assess service charges on the account(s) until you have nothing left.

There has been another interesting development in the area of bank service charges. I mention it here because of its relationship to what banks are doing to dormant accounts.

A sizable number of banks are now assessing monthly activity charges on savings accounts. There are varying ways these fees are derived. Some banks have a fee for each entry during the month. Some have a fee for "overuse" or "excessive" activity, as determined by the bank. Still others pay no interest if your balance is below one dollar. There is no universal review for me to present, as each bank has its own method for arriving at and assessing these fees.

This new attack on our savings is almost beyond comprehension. If we don't use our savings account, the bank calls it dormant, stops paying us interest, and starts charging monthly fees. At the other end of the spectrum, if we use our account, they charge us activity fees.

Let's see: low interest rates, dormant fees, activity fees, holds on deposits, long teller lines—no doubt about it, this is a deal you can pass.

ATMs

I've never liked automated teller machines (ATMs). For one thing, they were marketed in such a way as to exploit bank customers: ATMs were introduced as a free addition to a bank's services, but all along the industry planned that, once customers were separated from tellers, banks would start charging for the service. Now, as a result of this plan, ATM fees have skyrocketed and some banks are starting to charge a fee for being waited on by a real, live person. Imagine that!

Present fees for use of an ATM owned by your bank range from twenty-five cents to one dollar. But due to congressional complicity and recent changes in law, if you use a machine owned by another bank, you may be subject to an ATM surcharge—which could elevate your total expense per transaction to two dollars or more. This can get pretty expensive. For example, if you withdraw twenty dollars and are charged two dollars, the transaction cost you a 10 percent fee; mind you, that's 10 percent just to get your money. You're not borrowing anything, you're simply asking the bank for money you already have.

For some customers, the added convenience of an ATM is another easy way to spend more money than they should. Sadly, many people are almost addicted to ATM use.

ATM use can also create expensive overdrafts on joint accounts. If your spouse makes an ATM withdrawal that you don't know about, later in the day you may write a check (thinking you have funds) that ODs your account, hurts your credit rating with the firm that gets the bad check, and costs an OD fee of about twenty dollars. Of course, ODs caused by services that create confusion are designed by your bank for that very purpose.

ATMs are also a crime magnet. While the banks are not responsible per se, they should have culpability once a particular ATM has been hit a few times. How many customers have to be robbed and possibly assaulted before a bank either offers security or closes down the point? As ATMs are so profitable, the banks don't seem to care.

Don't forget the problems you'll have if your card or access number is lost or stolen. Read your agreement carefully. As many customers who have read their agreement *after* having a problem at an ATM can attest, it can be a real nightmare.

Last, when a bank in Chicago became the first to broach the possibility of charging a fee to see a teller, the result was outrage. It was a publicity fiasco of the first order. The local talk shows were inundated with incensed callers—"How dare they!" was the general theme. I shook my head and wondered why there was no such outrage regarding ATMs. It's the same principle, folks. You're being charged a fee to access money that you have been gracious enough to loan to your bank at low or no cost.

My advice? I wouldn't hesitate to use an ATM in an emergency. Short of that, it's just another rip-off.

Your Safe-Deposit Box Isn't So Safe

How safe is a bank safe-deposit box? Totally safe, most people would say. Sadly, the opposite is true. Bank safe-deposit boxes offer virtually no security. In fact, in some cases having a safe-deposit box will actually hinder the safety of your finances.

This is yet another perfect example of banks offering a service that is not what it purports to be; the consumer does not receive what he thought he purchased.

Most bankers, when asked about their safe-deposit function,

will tell you that their vault is impervious to theft, fire, and flood, and that no one, without your permission, can enter the box. Further, should the impossible happen, your contents are insured by the bank's insurance company, so there is no reason to worry. If you doubt this response, go to your bank and ask. You will find my scenario almost universally accurate.

If you believe your banker, a safe-deposit box sounds like a reasonable answer to the problem of protecting your valuables. It's too bad that's not the case. There are numerous potential problems with a bank safe-deposit box. As substantial as bank vaults are, a professional burglar can always get in if he or she so desires. Not so long ago a major money-center bank in San Francisco was burglarized. The thieves tunneled under all the security devices. Once inside, they short-circuited the electronic security. This bank's vault and security system were far in excess of what most community banks offer, and yet it was totally compromised. Having gained entry to the vault, a burglar can pop a safe-deposit box in about ten seconds using an ordinary screwdriver. That's what happened in this case.

A review of the facts makes it obvious that a safe-deposit box offers little substantive security. The only reason your bank's vault hasn't been victimized is that no professional thief has made an attempt. When and if that happens, the thief will be successful. So, the next time you get a warm feeling of security looking at your bank's vault, don't. It's more show than security.

Of course, your bank's vault doesn't have to be compromised for you to have problems. Floods and fire have to be considered.

A flood would not be too damaging under most circumstances, as the contents of the boxes would still be left intact. Damaged, maybe, but not lost. Fire, however, can be a major problem. Although the vault would normally be the last area to burn, it will burn. Therefore, the contents of your safe-deposit box may be lost if they are vulnerable to high temperatures. Stamp collections, paper money, important documents, and so on, will almost always be consumed.

Perhaps the biggest problem with a bank safety-deposit box is that if you have an unpaid delinquent tax obligation, the government, state or federal, can obtain a warrant to invade your box and confiscate its contents to pay the claim. The bank will have no choice but to comply with the warrant. If your safe-deposit box key is not available, or you will not voluntarily surrender it, the bank will have the lock drilled to assist the court officer. Then it will send you the bill for the drilling expense and a new lock for the box.

In many states, if you and your spouse (or another) have equal access to a safe deposit box and one of you dies, the bank will seal the box and not let the other enter under any circumstances. Even if the contents are valueless or belonged to you prior to your marriage, you will not be allowed access until the survivor provides the bank with all the appropriate state and/or federal tax releases. Meeting these documentation requirements can take weeks and, in some cases, months. This can become a tragic problem at a crucial time, especially if one has kept needed cash in the deposit box.

If the contents of your box are lost to fire or flood or are stolen, you're probably going to be surprised that you can't collect on the bank's insurance policy. Why? Because, unless you can prove to the satisfaction of the insurance company which contents were lost, you can't collect. That's what happened to many of the customers at the bank in San Francisco. They lost everything.

Proving a loss is impossible, by design of the bank and its insurance company. You see, your word is not enough. Nor is that of your family. Nothing you can say or do will convince the insurance company. An interesting paradox: The bank sells you a safe-deposit box and uses the advantage of confidentiality as a selling point. Then, when there is a problem, the bank's insurance company uses that confidentiality to deny legitimate claims.

Since I am strongly recommending that you don't use the bank's safe-deposit vault, here are some viable alternatives that offer the safety and security your bank box does not.

Consider a home safe. There are many available for under $250 that meet or exceed the fire rating of a bank vault. Proper location in the house would almost completely eliminate the possibility of flood damage. By obtaining the proper appraisals and a rider on your homeowners' insurance policy, you will have provided the insurance protection the bank doesn't offer. At the very least, if you do experience a loss, you'll have a chance of collecting a reimbursement. That's usually not true at the bank.

A home safe would not be any stronger than a bank vault, and therefore it, too, is susceptible to a break-in. But, only you will know where the safe is located, or even that you have one. An amateur won't be able to open your home safe, and there is little reason to expect that a professional thief would bother. The pros would rather expend their efforts on a bank vault, where hundreds of families have their valuables in one central location.

If you do rent a safe-deposit box, make sure it's located substantially outside your market area. The reasoning is this: A tax lien or warrant, for example, is good only if it is known where it should be served. In most cases, the government agency will check only the records of banks in your hometown and immediate surrounding communities. The remoteness of your safe-deposit box's location protects your assets and makes the warrant worthless.

The same reasoning holds true with a death. Your box won't be sealed if the bank is not aware that one of the owners has passed away, and that's unlikely if you're not well known in the town where you have your safe-deposit box.

In both examples I am not suggesting that you circumvent the law. My alternatives serve to show you how to avail yourself of your legal rights. If you have to travel a distance to use your safe-deposit box it may be inconvenient, but well worth the effort.

Another good alternative is to use private safe-deposit box companies. They are easy to locate; look in the Yellow Pages under "Safe-deposit boxes." They are worthy of consideration but can present some of the same problems a bank safety-deposit box does.

Finally, remember this: Use caution in deciding where you place your valuables. Don't find out the hard way that a bank safe-deposit box is misnamed.

You Can't Trust the Trust Department

There are many valid reasons why you might consider using a trust account. They can provide a number of important functions, from assisting in lowering your tax burden to help in caring for a disabled person. But the advisability of a trust isn't the issue.

The question here: Is a bank's trust department the right choice as your trustee?

Your decision should be one that gives control of your trust account to someone financially astute who understands your wants, needs, and expectations. In certain circumstances, you have the option of being your own trustee, but, in most instances, that's not the case.

For some smaller trusts, a friend or relative can perform quite well as trustee, provided he or she is given specific instructions. However, any individual, as opposed to an institution, has a drawback—continuity. Institutions offer longevity individuals can't. That shouldn't be forgotten.

Larger or more complicated trusts call for management by an expert. Here's where many get in trouble: They turn to their bank's trust department. Most money-center banks will not even consider a trust of less than $250,000. Hometown banks usually have a cutoff of fifty thousand dollars. Generally, the fees associated with a trust includes a setup charge, plus approximately 1 percent of the trust's worth per year as a maintenance fee. Associated transaction expenses are occasionally assessed.

The horror stories regarding bank trust departments are numerous. The biggest problem is that, if you get locked into an irrevocable trust, the trustee—regardless of how incompetent—will continue to have working control of the trust's assets. You can go to court to fight the issue, but, unless fraud can be proven, the courts generally side with the bank and let it continue to serve as trustee. Clearly, whether you choose a bank or not, an irrevocable trust can be dangerous. There are other, more flexible trust options available. Of course, if the trust was left to you by another, you have little choice.

Based on experience, I can say without hesitation that most community banks have trust departments whose staff are professionally unqualified. Too often they are supervised by someone fresh out of law school, or a longstanding bank employee who sees the trust department as a way to hide from the competition in the real world. Of course, there are exceptions.

Bigger banks present another problem. Unless your account is substantial (at least a million dollars, or close to it) it will get little hands-on supervision. Each trust officer may have two or three hundred accounts, which means there is little time available for the smaller trusts.

So you're faced with a dilemma. The smaller bank is too often incompetent, while the larger bank is too busy to give you the management necessary for good performance. Here are some better alternatives: Trust companies, trust attorneys, and trust accountants. To locate one, ask around. Word of mouth is probably the best way to find a good trust source. Regardless of whom you choose, you must do your homework and ascertain proof of the person's or institution's management results. Talk to others who use their services, and check with professional associations. You must have complete faith in your trustee. Keep shopping until you feel comfortable.

There is another, more important, issue regarding bank trust departments, and that is honesty. Unfortunately, some trust departments use their trusts as a cheap money pool for the bank's investment purposes. Little effort is given to maximizing the return to the trust accounts. Quite the contrary. Simply stated, instead of opting for safe, higher returns, they choose one of the bank's investment vehicles. And the lower the return the better. Better for the bank, not for the trust. Of course, the more money the bank's trust department can offer the bank's deposit function, the more money the bank has to invest in the lending function. And the less the bank has to pay for that money, the larger its profit margin. The lending function returns high rates for the bank's bottom line, while the trust's beneficiary may be receiving only the passbook rate for his or her account balance(s). Sadly, many bank trust departments see their responsibility in this light. And for this "professionalism," the bank then charges a yearly trust-maintenance fee on the account.

Perhaps you're thinking this scenario can't possibly be true. Sorry, it is nothing more than a proven statement of facts. The comptroller of the currency has in the past had to warn one hundred large U.S. banks to stop investing their trust monies in their own bank's passbook accounts. The banks in question were supposed to be investing these funds for the benefit of the trusts in safe, high-return investments. Yet, they were getting the lowest return possible, the passbook rate. The banks were purposefully mismanaging their trusts for their own benefit.

The government will do almost anything to protect banks from public scrutiny. That makes this admission from the comptroller's office even more alarming. When a government agency finally admits that a bank, or the banking industry, is guilty of an indiscretion, the actual scope of the problem is so acute that it can no longer be hidden. Further, what is known publicly is only the tip of the iceberg. The actual degree of such malfeasance may never be known, but at least the problem was finally admitted.

At the level of smaller community banks, because they receive even less government supervision, the problem expands. Worse yet, it has yet to be solved. Like so many banking-consumer issues, the government does as little as possible, and then hopes the public will forget.

Trusts are an excellent answer to many financial questions. You shouldn't ignore their value. However, I strongly suggest you avail yourself of your other trust options. Your bank's trust department may not be competent or trustworthy.

Debit Cards

A debit card is a checkless check. When you use your card, the amount of the transaction is immediately deducted from your checking account instead of being assessed against a credit card's line of credit. You don't even get the benefit of the check's taking a few days to clear. It's another small step toward the moneyless, checkless society bankers want so desperately.

I have three strong reservations regarding the use of debit cards. First, it's another attempt by the banking industry to encourage customers to spend money by making it easier to do so. That easy-access philosophy has gotten many consumers in trouble (for example, most personal bankruptcies include staggering credit-card debt).

Next, if you are married, a debit card may cause you to overdraw your account without knowing it. If you have a debit card and a personal identification number (PIN) along with your checking account, it's only a matter of time before confusion ensues between you and your spouse and an overdraft is created. Of course, the bank doesn't care. OD charges are one of their major money-producers, as we discussed earlier.

Finally, too many customers don't realize that a debit card is not a credit card, and the laws regarding losses due to illegalities are different. With a credit card, you're liable only for up to fifty dollars. With a debit card, you may be obligated up to five hundred dollars. In some cases, the loss could involve your checking-account balance and your maximum overdraft line of credit, and that could add up to a whole lot more than five hundred dollars.

If you have a debit card, did your bank make these facts clear to you? Again, I doubt it, because withholding vital information from consumers is the banking industry's stock-in-trade.

Brokerage Services

As banks branch out into new markets, beware. On the subject of brokerage services, last year's loan clerk may be this year's stock-market expert. Lack of expertise is too often the case especially at smaller banks.

Bigger banks are, of course, better staffed with people who have, at the minimum, adequate expertise to be of service.

My objection to using a bank's brokerage service at all is quite simple. If you need full-service brokerage help, a small bank usually is completely inadequate. If you're astute enough not to need full service, a big bank will do, but they're generally overpriced. Almost any discount brokerage house has a better fee schedule. Check it out, you'll see I'm right.

Banks want to expand their product base—not to be of more

service, but to generate more profits. I find no fault in that, as they are in business to make money. My objection is with their ad campaigns that swear the only reason they're in business is to be your friend. Nonsense.

Beyond that lie, as banks expand into new markets, the service they offer, whatever it is, is usually substandard because it's a sideline, and/or it's overpriced—and you could get a better deal consulting a professional who practiced in a specialized field 100 percent of the time for a long time.

Other Services

Your bank uses every opportunity to exploit your finances. The following two examples appear benign and inconsequential, but demonstrate the bank's propensity to exploit every opportunity to make huge returns on the daily transactions of an innocent, trusting, and unsuspecting public. Let's review money orders, cashier's checks, and traveler's checks to make the point once again.

Typically, each money order costs the consumer at least one dollar (you can do better than that at the post office; it charges only eighty-five cents). A cashier's check costs about two dollars. In many areas of the country the cost for both is higher. Even at lower prices, I want to prove to you, you are being abused if you use the bank for such daily financial needs.

Let's take this example: You are going to buy a used car. You purchase a cashier's check for five thousand dollars late on Wednesday afternoon. You close the deal on the car on Friday. The seller takes the check to his bank on Saturday. It clears back at the originating bank on the following Tuesday. That means the bank had the use of your five thousand dollars for six days, while at the same time charging you two dollars for the check. Now let's perform a cost analysis:

```
Cashier's Check for
    $5,000.00.............................(Fee) $2.00

Interest earned by bank
    ($5,000.00 × 12% × 6 days).................9.86
Total earned by bank............................11.86
Minus the cost of check printing....................0.15
Minus the cost of handling
    (computer and employee costs) ..................0.30
Net profit to the bank.........................$11.41
```

Note: The 12 percent interest rate is a fair representational consumer-loan rate. It could actually be lower, or higher.

This may sound like a small amount with which to concern ourselves but as a consumer you must realize that this one example, expanded by millions, gives an indication of how much money banks make on these "services" daily. Additionally, this same principle holds for money orders and traveler's checks. Banks make hundreds of millions of dollars by using the float in our small transactions. I have no objection to that, except that they won't allow us the same privilege when we make deposits. The bank's fees for any bank check, and virtually all other services, are completely unjustified. How unjustified? In our example, the bank expended a total of forty-five cents. It earned $11.41. That represents an interest-rate return to the bank of 2,536 percent.

I want to repeat that figure: 2,536 percent! And what are banks paying on our deposits? Once again, there seems to be a disparity. As with all bank income/consumer cost comparisons, that shouldn't come as much of a surprise.

Let's look at real-estate tax collection to understand this fully. Most of us pay our real-estate tax bill at the local bank. We do it either in person or through an escrow account. We have already discussed the latter. Let's look at the former.

In exchange for the convenience of being able to pay your taxes locally, your bank once again uses your money to its own benefit. The bank serves as an agent of the collector and remits those funds deposited at the bank directly to the tax office at predetermined times. In many large cities, the taxes are remitted almost daily. In most community banks (the largest number of commercial banks are in this category, i.e., small) the time available to the banks to use the monies collected varies from a few days to a few weeks to a few months. Let's use three weeks as typical.

Assuming a real-estate tax bill of $1,500, what income is the bank able to generate with your real-estate tax deposit? Remember, this issue is completely different from our previous escrow discussion.

Taxes collected.............................$1,500.00
Return to bank
      ($1,500 × 12% × 3 weeks) 10.38
Bank processing costs
      (computer and employee)......................0.50
Net to bank...................................$9.88

Here again, a small amount. However, to understand the impact of this principle, consider that this figure would naturally be multiplied by hundreds or thousands of tax bills, depending on the size of the town or city. That means the consumer base of this community lost whatever the bank made. Further, since the bank wasn't paying any interest to the county tax collector, the county lost, too. The only entity that prospers here is the bank. Banks are masters of making returns on the assets of others.

What return did the bank make on this service? In our example, it had a net profit of 1,976 percent.

I hope these quick, simple, everyday examples have helped make my point: Your bank will take every opportunity to take as much of your money as possible.

The problem is that because of the system, it's very hard, if not impossible, for a consumer to understand all the ramifications of any transaction. The banks have designed matters for that very purpose. If you did understand the real net cost to you (remember, if the bank made money using your funds, you were denied a return that was yours) you probably would never use a bank, or at the very least you would demand costs that were fair. And if that weren't possible, you would explore other options.

For instance, if you knew that your local gas station was making a return of 2,000 percent on a gallon of gas, would you patronize it? No, of course not. Yet that's what's happening when you patronize your local bank.

The basic problem, of course, is that with a bank you are dealing with an industry that is routinely guilty of what amounts to price-fixing. Banks don't have gas wars over service charges. That means the banking consumer is a captive audience. That's why the banking industry has fought so long and hard to ensure that "nonbank" banks can't enter their market. They know if real competition enters the field, their ability to deceive the consumer will be lost. For instance, aggressive "nonbank" banks would soon be offering money orders, cashier's checks, and traveler's checks for free or at lower cost than banks, as they would settle for the use of the "float" to make their profit. Meanwhile, the banking consumer must demand changes. The industry isn't going to stop overcharging on its own. There will have to be severe pressure exerted by individuals, consumer groups, and the government.

We, the very people that make the deposits, without which banks couldn't do business, have a right to be treated fairly. Service charges should be justifiable by cost analysis. If the bank prospers with our money, we have a right to share in that return. We could dissect each bank "service" with the same or like results.

I want to say again, point blank, that I am a conservative, free-market advocate. I believe that the government has no business in business. But, banks aren't part of any competitive free market. They have a government-sanctioned, taxpayer-subsidized monopoly. That changes all the rules. When they accept the benefits of a monopoly, they assume responsibility to those they serve. Unfortunately, that benefit/responsibility relationship has been lost, to the detriment of the consumer.

So the next time you think you're receiving a service from your bank, no matter the area, no matter the charge, be advised that you're being *over*charged, and the word "service" is being corrupted.

And What About...?

This handy short A-to-Z list covers those topics that didn't, by themselves, warrant a chapter, but are a necessary part of your banking education.

Why do you need this information in your banking arsenal? Because the assault by your bank on your finances has never been so focused and abusive as it is now. For example, according to the "Fee Income Report" newsletter, the number of different types of bank fees has risen from 96 in 1990 to over 250 in 1996. Another example: the Nader Group reports that the banking industry took in almost $2.6 billion in ATM fee revenue in 1994—while saving more than $2.4 billion in teller costs, because customers are using ATMs instead of tellers. Sadly, banks aren't satisfied with lowering expenses to increase profits: they want to reduce service, thereby lowering their costs, then increase the consumer's cost for this lesser service. They want a double dip. That's why you have to be prepared. This list will help.

APYs: Annual percentage yields were supposed to take the guesswork out of shopping for the best savings deal. As we discussed previously, banks had many ways of computing interest, so it was almost impossible for a depositor to know which account returned the most interest. You ended up comparing apples and oranges. Hence, in response to the outcry of decades of unfairness, APYs were created. Now, all you had to do was compare the APYs to know which vehicle was the best deal. Not so! As bankers do so well, they used this supposedly consumer-friendly law to exploit their customers. How is that possible? It's simple. They advertise an attractive APY, but add increased minimum-balance requirements (a subject reviewed shortly), fees, penalties, and other stipulations to make the actual APY substantially less than advertised. So when you're comparing APYs, which is a good idea, don't forget to compare all the nuances of the account that may take that attractive APY down to zero percent—or, worse yet, may mean you may actually owe money on an interest bearing account!

ATMs: While we've talked about ATMs, you should know what to do if you experience a problem with one. First, immediately contact a bank officer. The bank is required to give you the correct paperwork once it has had time to balance the machine for the day. It's also a smart thing to take notes so you remember exactly what took place and to whom you talked. As many customers can tell you, when an ATM makes an error—for instance, gives you the wrong amount of money—it can be a nightmare to correct the problem. Too often the bank treats you as if it was your fault that its machine didn't work.

Bank charges: We've talked about bank charges and fees in chapter after chapter, but there's one more important point. Often, when your account is assessed a fee for whatever reason, even a legitimate one, the bank throws your account into overdraft status without your knowledge. For example, it will deduct a research fee, a deposit-item return fee, an uncollected funds charge, and suddenly your small balance is a negative balance. By the time you receive the fee charge notice in the mail, you may have incurred two or three expensive ODs. Banks are notorious for this practice. They create overdrafts in your account, then make you pay for them. If your bank pulls this trick on you, demand your money back.

Bank errors: Banks make errors all the time. Each and every day, there are thousands of bank errors made on accounts throughout the country. As the bank has its intimidating reputation on the line with every mistake, it will do almost anything not to admit it's the bank's fault and, if possible, make the customer pay for its own unprofessionalism. Understanding this fact of banking life should give you the courage to demand fair treatment.

Don't be intimidated, regardless of what your banker says. If the bank made an error, it is obligated to fix it. For example, on checking account statements, many banks try and get around their responsibility by including wording to the effect of "This statement is presumed correct unless you notify the bank within thirty days." Notwithstanding, the bank cannot profit from its error. In most instances, it has to repay your money and any lost interest.

Bill paying: Many banks now offer a bill-paying service. I don't recommend it, because it's not wise to allow anyone, even your bank, unfettered access to your account. Besides, if the bank makes a mistake, you're the one who is going to be embarrassed, even though the bank must correct that error once it's brought to its attention. Then too, why pay someone for something you can and should do yourself?

Club accounts: Usually a bad deal. Never mind the marketing. When you're saving money, you want the best return on your investment, which usually means a club account of any kind (Christmas, vacation, and so on) is out.

Confidentiality: If you live in a metropolitan area, this issue probably isn't relevant. However, if you live in small town where everyone knows everyone else, it's critical that your bank respects the confidential nature of your banking relationship. If your banker(s) breach that trust and you can prove related damage, it's worth talking to an attorney. Certainly you should change banks if you suspect any improprieties.

Coin charges: Some banks now charge for coin counting and/or large coin requests. If your bank is one of them, and you need the service on a regular basis, find another bank. This is the equivalent of a restaurant charging you extra for a glass of water.

Credit rating: One of your most valuable assets is your credit rating. If your bank—or anyone else for that matter—makes a mistake in reporting your credit with that institution, and in so doing harms your credit rating, make the party correct it. There are numerous laws protecting a consumer so victimized and the bank knows that, so it will respond if you're assertive and let them know you understand the law.

Deposit-item return fee: You make a deposit. One of the checks in the deposit is returned. Your bank sends you a bill. What! You didn't do anything wrong. You didn't overdraft your account. If anything, you're a victim. Unpleasant as it is, your bank doesn't care—all they want is your money, and, as this outrageous charge proves, they're not too choosy as to how they get it. If you're charged a deposit item return fee, demand your money back. If the bank isn't receptive, find another bank.

Foreclosure: Don't be intimidated by a mortgage foreclosure. In most states, the bank must first go to court to prove legally that you're delinquent in your payments. Once that's done, the bank will hold an auction to sell your home to the highest bidder. The proceeds of the sale are applied to the remaining mortgage balance, with any excess going to you. If the house is sold for less than you owe, you may be sued for the difference.

A few words of caution. First, if you receive a foreclosure notice, call your lawyer immediately. If you can't afford one, call Legal Aid. You can't go up against the bank alone on this one. Next, never sign anything unless your lawyer approves. Many banks try and talk home owners about to lose their homes into signing away their rights—for example, their one-year redemption right (applicable in some states)—don't do it!

Finally, some banks cut "sweetheart" deals on many foreclosures. Even though the bank is obligated to get a fair price for the home, often the property is sold for just the amount of the mortgage, and the homeowner's equity "disappears" into the hands of the buyer, who too often has ties to the bank and/or one of the bankers. If you're losing your home to foreclosure, follow the transaction from start to finish. If there's something that appears wrong—for example, the home is sold for less than market value, contact your lawyer or the authorities.

Forgeries: Case law on forgeries is voluminous to say the least. Each case must be reviewed carefully to arrive at resolution. However, in a general sense, if the customer informs the bank of a forgery within fourteen days of discovering it, the bank is obligated to make restitution, because it is supposed to know the signatures of its depositors. This holds true for both checking and savings accounts.

If a paid forgery is large enough, the bank may refuse to return your money in the hope that you will take their word that you're culpable. If this happens to you, contact an attorney immediately.

Harassment: Banks often go over the line in collection situations even though the Fair Debt Collections Practices Act states that they cannot "harass, oppress, or abuse any person in connection with the collection of a debt."

If you feel the bank has gone too far, start taking notes of everything that happens. If you decide to file a complaint with the authorities and/or file a lawsuit, a complete record of events will help protect your rights.

If you even *feel* harassed, contact the Federal Trade Commission and all appropriate banking agencies—and if you know you're being harassed, contact a lawyer or Legal Aid.

Income-tax preparation: Here again, this is a sideline for your bank. As you are ultimately responsible for your tax return, regardless of who prepared it, it's best to go to a professional specializing in tax preparation.

And as for those banks that employ a professional service that simply sets up shop in the bank's lobby at tax time, they're probably going to charge you an exorbitant fee because, once again, the bank makes money as a middleman. Save money—go directly to the source.

Minimum balances: Minimum balances are the bane of the average checking account. The fees charged on them can, as mentioned previously, completely negate any interest earned on an account. Sadly, banks arrive at minimum balance requirements by auditing their checking account deposit base to determine what minimum figure will force the most customers to fall below the balance set, thereby generating income for the bank while at the same time allowing the bank to advertise a "competitive" APY. The fact that the average minimum balance requirement has escalated to a whopping $1,500 (up from $300 since deregulation), while the average return on a NOW (negotiable order of withdrawal) account has dropped to approximately 1.5 percent (down almost 70 percent since deregulation) proves the point.

Mortgage insurance: Mortgage insurance is a decreasing term policy that pays the bank the remaining mortgage balance should the insured die. Like credit-life insurance on an installment loan, mortgage insurance payouts go directly to the bank instead of being accessible to the customer for use in any purpose your family may choose. Then too, in some instances the bank has a relationship with the actual insurer, which increases your costs because (here we go again) the bank becomes an expensive middleman.

A better deal: buy a decreasing-term insurance policy from an independent insurance agent in an amount and term equal to your present mortgage and term. This accomplishes the same end as the vehicle the bank may be offering, but it gives your family flexibility at a reduced price.

Night drop: Never use your bank's night drop unless your deposit consists solely of checks that can be replaced and are signed with a restrictive endorsement (for example: "For deposit only in account #15 375 8"). As many customers can attest, sometimes night-drop deposits "disappear," and when that happens, as the bank won't make restitution for unverified deposits—the depositor is out that portion of the deposit that cannot be replaced—such as cash. As you can see, the convenience of the night drop can become very expensive.

Overdrafts: One more word on this important "service." Banks will do almost anything to increase the profit in this, one of their major profit centers, and that includes the unconscienable act of arbitrarily selecting which checks are returned or paid on the basis of what's best for the bank. For example, say you write five checks in the amounts of $300, $100, $100, $50, and $50 that OD your account $250. Some banks, instead of returning the one check for three hundred dollars that would solve the problem and only cost you only a twenty dollars fee will return two one-hundred dollars checks and one fifty dollars check—charging for three ODs and thereby generating three times the profit for the bank. Make sure this isn't happening to your account.

PMI insurance: Private mortgage insurance (PMI) is required by some lenders when the borrower isn't able to meet the down-payment requirement on a mortgage purchase. For example, if the bank requires a 30 percent down payment but you have only 18 percent, the bank may make the loan if you'll insure them, through a PMI policy, for the 12 percent differential.

The biggest problem with PMI is that often it is not cancelled when you finally meet the down payment requirement, through monthly payments and/or inflationary rise in the worth of the property. Don't depend on the bank to tell you when you can cease paying for this expensive policy or you'll end up paying premiums for the life of the loan. When you think you may have met the original requirements, talk to your banker about cancellation.

Participation loans: As you know from reading this far, I favor smaller banks over the impersonal monoliths. We've discussed the reasons. But there is one problem with smaller banks. Often they don't have a loan limit that will meet the needs of some of its larger business customers. If your loan request is denied on this basis, remind your banker about his ability to be the lead bank in a participation loan. Simply put, a number of banks can band together to meet your needs. You'll only have to maintain contact with your bank, so this isn't as confusing as it may seem. If, after being reminded of this option, the banker still turns you down, you'll know that your banker wasn't telling you the truth—he or she just used the loan limit as an excuse.

Another lending excuse is that "the loan committee turned you down"—the banker didn't, it was the fault of the faceless loan committee. While it is true that banks have loan committees, they are reserved for loans far beyond the needs of the average consumer.

If your bank isn't being up front with you regarding your loan requests (I'm going to say it again), find another bank.

Past-due-loans: Never let a loan become past due, especially if it's your mortgage. The moment you realize you have a problem, go to the bank and explain what's happening. Usually, something can be worked out. Perhaps you can arrange a loan extension of a few months until your financial situation improves.

By being straightforward you not only can save your house or car if it was the collateral, you can also save your credit rating.

Unfortunately, most customers who are having problems do exactly the wrong thing. They start making excuses or promises they can't keep, when they should simply be honest and tell the bank why they can't make their payment, and then work out a schedule of delayed repayment that both they and the bank can accept.

Penalties: Since deregulation, banks have a penalty for everything—it's a huge income-generating source. Protect your accounts and ask for unjustified penalties to be returned.

We've talked about loan late charges before, so this time let's focus on savings accounts, specifically a bank certificate of deposit (CD). When you make an early withdrawal at some banks, you may find that not only have you lost all your interest, you may have lost a portion of your principal as well. The penalty can be that egregious—so before you make a deposit in a CD, or establish any account relationship with a bank, make sure you understand exactly what the account's penalties can cost you. Don't get so wrapped up in shopping for the best APY that you lose it all by failing to understand the entire contract.

Repossessions: Never, and I mean never, sign away any of your rights as a lending consumer.

Many states have very strong consumer-protection laws that preclude the bank from repossessing your car—unless it can convince you, somehow, that you must sign certain paperwork. Paperwork that you may not understand can waive your rights. Unless you want to give the car back to the bank, call your lawyer and/or Legal Aid or your state's consumer protection agency (usually located in the capital).

Research fees: As I've said before, banks are perhaps the only "service" businesses that believe they deserve an outrageous fee every time they lift a finger to help one of their customers. Research fees are a case in point.

For example, many banks no longer return your checks with your monthly statement (some return a small picture of your checks). This saves the bank filing costs, as well as postage fees. You'd think the bank would be happy about this rather substantial improvement in its bottom line, but no, once again the banks want more. They won't return your checks (remember, these are *your* checks—you paid for them) and if you need a copy of one, to rectify a disputed bill for example—they send you a bill for about three dollars as a research fee. Again, they create a problem (by not returning your checks) and then profit handsomely from the reduction in service.

Stop payments: Don't bother paying fifteen dollars or so for a stop-payment order for a check worth about the same amount—especially if the check was written to a respectable person or business where your odds of resolving a dispute are good.

Also, when you purchase a stop payment, read the fine print carefully. There are exclusions that protect the bank if your check gets paid—you may not find them acceptable.

Last, if a bank makes an error in paying a large check that was stopped, it may try to avoid reimbursing your loss, hoping that you don't understand your rights or won't be willing to "fight city hall," so to speak. Don't be intimidated. Demand your money back.

Traveler's checks: Traveler's checks are too expensive to be worth purchasing, not to mention the fact that you're allowing the issuing company use of your float until each check clears. A better bet now that technology has made traveler's checks almost obsolete; use your credit card to get a cash advance. While I don't recommend cash advances under normal circumstances, in this case, as long as you have a card that doesn't charge interest if your bill is paid in full each month, all you're looking at is a transaction fee.

Uncollected funds: Much of the time, when a customer receives an uncollected-funds charge (remember, here you haven't really overdrafted your account), it's an exceptional rip-off, because the money you deposited *was* collected (almost all checks clear within forty-eight hours), even though the bank is saying otherwise. The reason this seeming contradiction occurs is that, as previously mentioned, the EFAA now uses business days instead of calendar days to calculate its check-clearing requirements.

If the bank receives credit for our deposits within forty-eight hours, then our accounts should receive a like credit at the same time, not days later. If we make a deposit on Monday, it shouldn't get posted on Tuesday simply because the bank has set a cutoff time of 2 P.M. for its own convenience. Again, this sleight-of-hand is a huge income producer for the bank. It gets to use our money interest free and charge us a fee too.

If you get an uncollected-funds charge when you know you made a deposit on time, ask for your money back.

Most important, allow this subject to make clear the fact that when you're dealing with your bank, it has two sets of rules, and one set is completely unfair to the very people that allow the bank to stay open—its depositors.

Conclusion

At the start of this book, I challenged you to reserve judgment on my statement that your bank is an enemy. It's time for your answer. I believe that you are left with no choice but to conclude that I am right.

Frankly, because I care so much about the consumer, I wish I were wrong. I take no pride in acknowledging that a system in which I strongly believe, the banking system, is abusing the very people that allow this system to function in the first place. Bankers have purposely forgotten that without the customer-depositor they have no bank. Every customer is important, and by that very fact he or she deserves respect and fair consideration. You and I know banks don't believe that. Their actions speak louder than their words and false advertisements.

Sadly, things will likely get worse. Deregulation, the worst thing that ever happened to the bank consumer since the Depression, has exacerbated the problem. Instead of allowing real competition in the marketplace, deregulation is offering the consumer progressively fewer, more costly choices. The big banks are buying up the little banks, giving the consumer fewer opportunities to comparison shop. In the last ten years the number of commercial banks has decreased 23 percent. Less competition isn't good for the banking consumer. Not only that, the bigger a bank gets, the less responsive it is to the needs of the individual. Look at the record. Deregulation has given the consumer exactly what? I'll tell you: Less service at four times the price, that's what.

Bankers and Congress want bigger and bigger money-center banks. They believe, judging by their actions, that there is no place for the community bank, and that fewer and fewer banks and bankers should control more and more of the nation's resources. They're wrong.

Based on the record, why should we, the banking consumers, trust bankers with our deposits? They can't handle their own business; Why should we entrust them with ours? And yet, Congress is consistently giving the banks more and more monopolistic concessions; bigger, broader, and better tax breaks; new markets (including underwriting, insurance, and real estate); and isolation from corporate competition. It seems that the more banks mismanage their business and our deposits, the better things get—for them, not us. We're paying more for less each and every day.

Bankers know that they are completely isolated from true free-market forces. The government's actions (the S&L bailout, for instance) make it clear that it pays financial institutions to take big risks with our money. If the bank is big enough, the government won't let it fail like other businesses are forced to do. That means banks can abuse their customer base without fear of the ultimate retribution, bankruptcy.

The fact is, banks are getting this country into deep trouble. They have a stranglehold on the economy. They have a stranglehold on the government. That means they have a stranglehold on us.

Yet, as important as that is, that's not the thrust of my message. If you learned nothing else from this book, the most important thing to remember is that your bank and banker is your enemy, and should be treated as such. They need us more than we need them, but they don't know that. So we have to understand how they play the game. They will take as much of your money as you allow them to take.

Because of this you must explore all your options. Don't just blindly follow what the banker says. The truth is, in a technical sense, most bankers aren't very good at their job. Want proof? Go in and ask your banker to explain exactly how they compute the Rule of 78s on an installment loan or the compound savings interest on day of deposit to day of withdrawal, compounded and paid daily. Don't settle for verbal tap-dancing. Demand a specific, documented answer. Chances are, your banker won't be able to give you one, because he doesn't know. Bankers know how to overcharge you for services, but past that, their knowledge is severely limited. That's what they have their almighty computers for. You know, the ones that never make mistakes.

An objective review of any banking relationship brings one to the inescapable conclusion that the bank will either use you, or you'll use it. It's up to you. In those instances where you can't get the banking service you want at the price you want, exercise one of your many other options. You don't have to do all your banking at a bank. You should use one only when it's profitable to do so.

It's amazing to me that people who will travel across town to save ten cents on a gallon of gas, or five cents on a can of peas, don't bother to shop for a bank. Actually, you should shop each banking service, not just the bank, as the banker's concept of a single bank being your "financial supermarket" is a con and hazardous to your wealth. A bank can take more money from you in a minute than the grocery store or gas station could take in a lifetime, and yet, no one bothers to exercise consumer caution when dealing with a financial institution.

How do banks get away with it? They spend time, money, and effort ensuring their position. They have lobbied long and hard for the legislative right to rip off their customers. They spend time, money, and effort creating an image and atmosphere that intimidates the consumer. They spend time, money, and effort ensuring that no others can enter their monopoly and create true competition for your business.

I am not trying to be hard on the banking industry. It may sound that way, but sometimes the truth hurts. There have been times when the industry has tried to argue my position with me. I have done many radio shows where I debated another banker. Each and every time, based on audience reaction, I clearly won. Why? I admit honestly that my debating skills are not that good, but my position is. There isn't a banker in the world who can justify the charges a bank assesses for an overdraft. There isn't a banker in the world who can deny that illegal bank officer transactions have adversely affected so many banks. There isn't a banker in the world who can dispute that taxpayers are subsidizing billion-dollar banks through the tax system and outright grants to the World Bank and International Monetary Fund. There isn't a banker in the world who can deny that FDIC reserves, even with the improvements of the last few years, are inadequate. There isn't a banker in the world who can justify making families give multibillion-dollar banks an interest-free loan by putting unreasonable hold times on their deposits. There isn't a banker in the world who can deny the setting of the prime interest rate isn't price fixing. I could go on, but you get the point. I won the debates because the bankers are in an indefensible position.

The fact of the matter is, banks, and the bankers that run them, know they are your enemies. They just hope you never realize it.

Contacting the Author

To reach me, write to Reliance Enterprises, Inc., P.O. Box 413, Marengo, Illinois 60152.

APPENDIX

How to Solve a Problem with Your Bank

It is becoming more and more difficult to find banking services that are worth the money, and/or a bank that cares about its customers. It seems that fewer and fewer bankers believe in the adage that the customer is always right. In short, your chances of being dissatisfied with your bank have increased dramatically during the last few years. It will help if you're prepared for this almost certain eventuality.

Some banking problems are simple, some are not. If your bank is typical, solving the dispute will be more difficult than you could imagine, whatever the circumstances. For some reason, banks feel they are above dealing with the normal concerns of a service business. Consequently, they are not as consumer-responsive as one would expect. To the contrary, rather than solving matters they often make the situation much worse.

The surest test of a bank's ability to meet the grandiose claims of its advertisements is how it reacts when there is a difficulty or dispute. Any bank can be friendly when things are going smoothly, but few meet their service claims when a customer has a problem.

Of course, the best way to avoid a problem with your bank is to do preventive maintenance prior to one occurring. To that end, you should bank at the smallest, or one of the smaller institutions in your market area. The small bank wants to become a big bank, and the way it accomplishes that goal is to have large number of satisfied customers. Many big banks erroneously believe they don't need the average customer, and their attitude reflects that thinking. In short, they don't care if you're unhappy or have a problem. They have a "we-do-it-our-way-or-we-don't-do-it-at-all" attitude.

Next, after establishing your account, it's wise to introduce yourself to as many of the bank officers and staff as possible. Make sure you meet the president, cashier, and chief loan officer. These three will be able to solve most, if not all, of your bank problems. The head of bookkeeping and head teller are two other individuals that shouldn't be overlooked, as they are the frontline people who may solve a problem before you are forced to seek a bank officer.

If you do have a problem, direct it up the proper chain of command. This alone can save you wasted time and effort. One of the reasons customers get "the banker's shuffle" (moved from desk to desk without satisfaction) is that they often start out in the wrong department when they first ask for assistance. The following list of chains of command will help the bank help you:

1. Teller; head teller; cashier; vice president for operations; executive vice president; president; board of directors

2. Loan clerk; loan officer; vice president for loans; executive vice president; president; board of directors

3. Bookkeeper; department head; cashier; vice president for operations; executive vice president; president; board of directors

These are the basic chains of command you'll need to know. The individual titles may vary, but not enough to be confusing. Here are a few examples to show how using the chain of command works. If you have a problem with a check returned against your account, where should you turn? Start with the department that issued the notice, which in this case would be bookkeeping. Begin with a bookkeeper and work your way up until receiving satisfaction. Don't give up, as a tactful, yet aggressive bank consumer can almost always get his or her way. The bottom line is,

Be assertive to the point where you will settle for nothing less than a fair resolution. After all, that's what the bank is supposed to offer in the first place. Another example: The bank won't let you cash a third-party check. Start with the chain that begins with a teller. Loan problems? Obviously, start with a loan clerk.

If you control the situation, start in the proper chain of command, politely demand results, and are willing to go to the board of directors if necessary, you'll normally be rewarded with positive results. But what happens when that doesn't work? It depends on the severity of the difficulty.

You might start with a letter to your state consumer affairs office and/or the Better Business Bureau.

If that doesn't work, you always have legal recourse. I won't address a major legal battle here, as that requires representation from an attorney who specializes in financial litigation. For other, less complicated cases, though, small claims court is the battlefield of choice. For example, if you've been assessed an overdraft fee in error and the bank won't return the charge, once it is served with papers, the bank will probably decide that it's better to comply with your request than spend perhaps ten times the OD charge to argue. Then, too, most banks don't want the potential embarrassment of having a number of bank officers trying publicly to explain a depositor's complaint in front of a judge and/or jury. For details regarding small claims in your state, ask your local court clerk for an informational brochure.

Also, there are a number of fine, inexpensive reference books about small claims court. Ask at your bookstore. One that I have found useful is *Everybody's Guide to Small Claims Court*, by Ralph Warner (Nolo Press, P.O. Box 544, Occidental, CA 95465).

Knowing how to use small claims court is important, since almost all your banking problems that can't be resolved at the bank can be solved through this forum. And, since many states don't allow lawyers in small claims court, your chances of a fair hearing are greatly enhanced. In these states, it's just you against your banker, one on one.

Lastly, don't overlook the option of arbitration. This presents an excellent, cost-efficient way of resolving almost any matter.

Arbitration panels are normally composed of experts in their fields, and many won't allow lawyers into the process. (To explore this option further, look in the Yellow Pages under "Arbitration.")

Perhaps the worst consequence of banking's unprofessionalism is that, as consumers, we have come to accept the fact that we pay more for less every day. The system is too huge and complex for us to fight, so we pay the outrageous bills, whatever the dispute, no matter who is right or wrong, and chalk it up as a lost cause. That's the attitude your banker wants you to have, because it's the wrong attitude. My banking and consulting experience make clear that an aggressive consumer almost always wins a viable case. Yes, it takes time and effort, but those who succeed are repaid on many levels. You can't afford to waste your hard-earned money. Never let a banker present you with a bill for anything other than legitimate professional service.

Unfortunately, bank/banker arrogance has bullied the public into believing: (1) Banks don't make errors (2) whatever the problem, it's your fault (3) you have to pay for the error regardless of who's responsible and (4) banks can't be beaten in an adversarial proceeding. All four are misconceptions.

Another sometimes-viable suggestion is approaching government agencies for help. It has been my experience that government agencies do as little as possible to assist a financial consumer, as I mentioned earlier. However, if you're aggressive, dedicated, and tenacious you can produce results, because many banks, once they realize you're serious, may decide to help you rather than have to write a number of letters to Washington. Results, therefore, come not from government intervention or law enforcement, but from creating aggravation for the banker. The following directory is a means to that end.

1. The White House
   Washington, D.C. 20500
   (202) 456–1414
2. Your Senator
   Senate Office Building

Washington, D.C. 20510
(202) 224–3121

3. Your Congressperson
House Office Building
Washington, D.C. 20515
(202) 224–3121

4. For problems pertaining to your mortgage loan, contact:
Department of Housing and Urban Development
    451 Seventh Street SW
    Washington, D.C. 20024
    (202) 755–6420

5. If you feel your financial institution has broken any law as it pertains to your account(s), contact:
    Department of Justice
    Tenth Street and Constitution Avenue NW
    Washington, D.C. 20530
    (202) 633–2000

6. If your bank has discriminated against you and/or you believe you have been denied credit due to race, color, national origin, sex, marital status, or age, contact:
    Department of Justice
    Civil Rights Division
    Tenth Street and Constitution Avenue NW
    Washington, D.C. 20530
    (202) 633–2151

7. If you are a victim of a fraud perpetrated by a financial institution, contact:
    Department of Justice Fraud Hot Line
    Tenth Street and Constitution Avenue NW
    Washington, D.C. 20530
    (202) 633–3365

8. For all problems and/or complaints involving a national bank (those banks with the word *national* in their name), contact:
    Comptroller of the Currency
    Administrator of National Banks

Washington, D.C. 20219
(202) 447–1750

9. If any problem with your bank affects your taxes, contact:
Internal Revenue Service
1111 Constitution Avenue NW
Washington, D.C. 20002–6433
(202) 566–4743

10. For any problem with a national or state bank, contact:
The Senate
Banking, Housing and Urban Affairs
534 Dirksen Building
Washington, D.C. 20510
(202) 224–7391

11. For any problem with a national or state bank, contact:
The House of Representatives
Banking, Finance and Urban Affairs
2129 Rayburn Building
Washington, D.C. 20515
(202) 225–4247

12. For any problem with a national or state bank, contact:
Board of Governors of the Federal Reserve
Federal Reserve Building
Washington, D.C. 20551
(202) 452–3000

13. For any problem with a bank that offers FDIC insurance, contact:
Federal Deposit Insurance Corporation
550 17th Street NW
Washington, D.C. 20006–4801
(202) 389–4221

14. For any problem regarding a savings and loan association, contact:
Office of Thrift Supervision
1700 G Street NW
Washington, D.C. 20552
(202) 906–6000

Savings Association Insurance Fund (SAIF)
550 17th Street NW
Washington, D.C. 20429
(202) 898–3542

15. For any problem with a bank that is a member of the Federal Reserve System, contact:

Federal Reserve System
20th Street and Constitution Avenue NW
Washington, D.C. 20551–0999
(202) 452–3684

16. For any problem with your bank stock and/or any brokerage transaction your bank may have processed, contact:

Securities and Exchange Commission
450 5th Street NW
Washington, D.C. 20001–2719
(202) 272–2650

17. For problems in acquiring a Small Business Administration (SBA) guarantee from your bank, and/or any problems with your SBA loan, contact:

Small Business Administration
1441 L Street NW
Washington, D.C. 20005–3524
(202) 653–6823

18. For your state banking authority's address and phone number, call local directory assistance. Normally this agency is located at the state capital. You should contact the agency for all problems regarding banks that do not have the word *national* in their name.

19. For information and advice regarding other appropriate federal agencies that may be able to offer consumer aid, call local directory assistance and ask for your nearest Federal Information Center. This agency will give you assistance and direction.

20. I believe your "best" government assistance can be garnered from your congressperson, as representatives are more sensitive to the importance of individual voter's needs. For the fastest, best, and most productive response, contact the congressperson's local district office. The address and number are listed in the phone book. If possible, make a personal visit to present your grievance.

21. If you need a lawyer's assistance, and you don't current employ one, contact your local American Bar Association's Lawyer Referral Service and describe the details of your problem. The service will recommend an attorney specializing in the legal requirements of your case. The number is available through directory assistance.

22. Don't forget your local state agencies, such as the State's Attorney's Office, the state Justice Department, the Office of Consumer Fraud. All of the phone numbers are either in the phone book or are available through directory assistance.

Banking Alternatives

Checking and savings accounts and loans are the most basic of banking services. However, as explained throughout this book, perhaps your bank isn't the best place to acquire these services. Here are some alternatives:

Checking:

Savings and loan associations have lower service charges than banks. Additionally, they have, on average, lower minimum-balance requirements.

Credit unions are another low-cost alternative. Their "checks," called draft shares, are often service-charge free. Those few that do apply a service charge to checking accounts have fees much lower than most banks. If they have a minimum balance requirement, it is normally around three hundred dollars instead of the average $1,500 at most banks. Their interest on checking accounts is generally one-half to one percentage point higher than banks pay. Not all credit unions have draft shares, so you may have to shop to find one in your area that does. To find a credit union you can join, call the Credit Union National Association at (800) 358-5710.

Service-charge-free accounts are available at most banks. If you're under eighteen, retired, a student, disabled, or over sixty-five, ask if your bank will provide a checking account at no charge. Almost all banks, savings and loans, and credit unions provide this service—but it is seldom advertised or offered without being requested.

Brokerage-house accounts in addition to asset management and brokerage services, offer checking-account privileges at no or low charge. However, they may charge a substantial fee to open the account, and/or a yearly fee to maintain it, so you must balance your savings against the annual fees to see your true bottom line.

Money-market mutual funds are another possibility, depending on your check-writing needs. As many have a minimum dollar requirement (for example, each check must be written for at least $250), they may not meet your needs. If you can live with their prerequisites, the cost is minimal.

No-frills checking accounts are offered by many banks and savings and loans. They have no minimum balance requirements, but often have a maximum on the number of checks you can write during a month. Your cost, provided you don't exceed the bank's activity limits, is a flat fee of two to five dollars per month. Each bank or savings and loan has its own particulars, so, as always, it pays to shop.

Low-cost checks can be purchased for about half the cost of checks purchased through your bank. It's one of banking's many dirty little secrets that they earn a profit on checks even though they're not the supplier. To order checks, call Current at (800) 426-0822 or Checks in the Mail at (800) 733-4443. Both companies guarantee their checks will meet all industry standards.

Savings:

Money-market mutual funds, in addition to being a possible checking-account alternative, should be considered from a savings standpoint. If you want added safety with this account, stick with those funds that invest only in Treasury Bills.

Tax-exempt money market funds are an even better answer, especially if you're in the higher income-tax bracket. The effect of taxes cannot be ignored when investing in a savings vehicle. You may be able to lessen your states income tax's impact on your total tax obligation by investing in a tax-exempt money market fund that invests in municipal securities in your state. Lowering or negating your tax on an investment is worth investigating.

Brokered CDs, while not necessarily good for the economic well-being of the country, are an excellent vehicle for maximizing your return. The broker shops rates nationwide and gets the best available that offers FDIC insurance. Brokered money contributed to the S&L crisis, but that's not germane, as it was a symptom, not a cause. As long as you're dealing with a respectable broker, brokered CDs can offer substantially larger returns than those offered at your local institutions.

Treasury securities are perhaps the safest consumer savings investment. The choice of vehicle is quite varied, from twenty-five dollars savings bonds, Treasury notes and bills, to issues that require a minimum investment of one million dollars.

Treasury investments can be purchased through your broker, many banks, or directly from the nearest Federal Reserve Bank. For a free booklet on how to purchase Treasury securities directly, write: Federal Reserve Bank of Richmond, Public Services Department, Box 27622, Richmond, VA 23261.

Here, too, the tax consideration is important, as Treasury securities are exempt from state and local taxes.

Nonbank banks have to be considered in today's aggressive market. Sears' Discover card account offers a savings plan, as do Household Financial Services, Beneficial Finance, and others. Credit unions also are worthy of your consideration. Their rates usually are competitive, and are insured by the National Credit Union Share Insurance Fund.

Loans:

Credit unions generally loan money at lower interest rates than do banks. Additionally, their loans fees are reduced or nonexistent. Terms are often more flexible.

Savings and loan associations, like credit unions, generally have lower interest rates and loan fees.

Insurance companies are often overlooked by policy holders. If you want to borrow money, call your insurance agent and see what he can do for you. Insurance companies have broadened their loan base, so it is likely they will have a plan for your personal borrowing needs. Here too, rates are usually lower than those at banks, often substantially so. Loan fees are often not assessed.

GMAC, Ford Motor Credit and other product manufacturers. I don't usually recommend obtaining loans from lending extensions of a product manufacturer, as they are usually a bad deal. But as you've no doubt noticed, GMAC and other companies often offer excellent terms for credit. Of course, they are doing so to sell more cars, but who cares? A 2.9 percent APR is a good deal when buying a car. These deals are hard to beat, and are not to be confused with a dealer's arranging financing at the local bank (where the dealer gets a percentage of the deal, thereby costing you more money).

One word of warning. Don't, in order to get the low-cost APR, agree to credit life and disability insurance. As noted earlier, it's a rip-off. Grab the low APR while demanding the stripped-down version of loan terms.

Private money is the most-often-overlooked source of funds. There is nothing that prohibits me, as a private investor, from being your mortgage holder, for example. Why private money? The rewards are numerous. A private mortgage usually has a lower interest rate (we've already discussed how even a small reduction in rate extrapolates to tens of thousands of dollars); low or no closing costs; no associated fees (secretary costs, bank lawyer fees, appraisal costs, credit application fees, and so on); lower down-payment requirements; and more flexible terms.

Where do you find private money? Call your broker, accountant, or lawyer and ask if they have any private-investor clients that loan money directly to individuals. If you don't have a lawyer, accountant, or broker, look through the phone book and start making cold calls.

I have never found anyone who couldn't locate private mortgage or business money provided they were aggressive and had a viable loan request.

Mortgages:

There was a time not too long ago when a mortgage was a mortgage. It had a fixed rate, a fixed term, and was easy to understand. As we've discussed, those days are gone.

The reason? As reviewed in the section on ARMs, financial institutions don't want long-term loan agreements. They believe they are too risky, considering the market fluctuations over the last decade. Most banks are poorly managed, and don't plan properly. It's much easier to make the consumer pay for the bank's shortcomings (i.e., isolate themselves from the market by introducing mortgage rates that are movable and retain the bank's profit margin regardless of events).

In response, some new types of mortgage arrangements have been introduced by creative sellers. Then too, some buyers saw the need for creative thinking, and made offers to purchase contingent on some financial lending participation on the part of the seller.

To make a long story short, the simple mortgage transaction, for a variety of reasons, is a thing of the past. I have no quarrel with that, as one should always explore all the financial options available. However, exercise caution. Remember the importance of your mortgage investment. There is no room for error! Remember, statistically, every home in America is sold every three to five years. Keeping up on your mortgage education is therefore required.

It's critical that you understand all your options. To that end, in addition to the general loan alternatives listed above, I offer these alternatives to the standard mortgage.

Land contract: Here, the seller becomes the mortgage holder; title doesn't transfer until principal is paid in full. The interest rates for land contracts are usually below market, which is a plus. My reservations are based on the fact that, since the title doesn't transfer until the debt is paid, the buyer has very little protection if there is a problem during the loan's term. The buyer has no land equity until the title transfers, which may also be a problem. I have no quibble with the principle behind a land contract; in fact,

I recommend it. However, where most get hurt is having a poorly structured or misunderstood contract.

Rent with option to buy: The renter pays a fee for an option price of X dollars some time in the future. Ideally rent, or a portion thereof, would go toward the purchase price. This form of purchase may be ideal for those who would not, under normal circumstances, be able to buy a property they desire. At the end of the option there may be financing problems, but that's not the fault of the option principle. Exercise caution, get a fair option price, and you should be satisfied with the results.

Equity conversion loan: The borrower currently owns property and has a need for additional income (this vehicle is usually marketed to the elderly). The lender makes payments to the borrower using the property as collateral. Although it can provide cash to the borrower, this form of loan more often that not is a short-term solution to a long-term problem. At the end of the term, the borrower must repay in full, or refinance. But the chances of refinance are slim. If the borrower had income that would allow for a standard mortgage, he wouldn't have taken out this type of loan in the first place. The bottom line? A forced sale is the only out. This is a risky option.

Assumable mortgage: The buyer takes over the seller's present mortgage (usually below market rate), by paying the difference between the selling price and mortgage balance to the seller in cash, or through a seller second mortgage. This is good for the seller, and good for the buyer. However, many new mortgages will not allow anyone else to assume the mortgage. Be alert to this when you sign your mortgage at closing. You will want to retain assumability, as it will help you sell your property, should you desire.

Seller second: The seller provides all or part of the purchase-price mortgaging through a first or second mortgage. This plan is usually associated with below-market interest rates. As long as the buyer can afford the additional monthly expense, and does not allow himself to get into a "balloon trap," this method of financing can be extremely profitable. Make a mistake though, and you've probably lost the property.

Shared appreciation: This usually involves a below-market rate in exchange for a portion of the property equity when the property is eventually sold. There are many variations on this theme, and it is a haven for those who appreciate creative financing. For instance, through this method, a family may decide to help their parents (or the parents, their children) purchase a property or keep the one they have. In this case, the financing has merit. If you're "buying in" with an independent financer you may have problems. For instance, if the property increases in equity beyond expectations due to inflation, or appreciation, you may end up paying a very steep price to your "partner." Some agreements contain a clause whereby the property must appreciate a certain percentage or you will owe additional monies. Use caution!

Wraparound: The buyer is able to use the seller's low interest rate on his present mortgage. The seller takes payments from the buyer and forwards the mortgage payment to the mortgage holder while keeping the difference for himself. The difference is the amount amortized for the actual mortgage and the amortization amount necessary to complete the purchase. Dangerous legal ramifications can arise here. For example, the buyer can lose his equity if the seller "defaults" to the mortgage holder.

Buy-down: This is usually a developer's marketing tool. He subsidizes your monthly payments for a predetermined time, which allows you, the buyer, to buy in on property you otherwise couldn't afford. As long as you know you can "pay the freight" when the subsidy term has expired, and there are no hidden fees for the subsidy, you may find you can make or save money with this one. If you actually *need* the subsidy, stay away.

Creative financing is the name of the game. It can work for you; it can work against you. If used correctly, it can help stop the bank and others from abusing your finances. The key is education. If you have questions, consult an attorney.

New mortgage alternatives are being introduced in the market all the time. Then too, if you can conceive it, chances are you can finance it. Be creative.

Small-Business Loans:

This book is devoted to the individual banking consumer, not businesses. However, I know many of you may own your own small business. This section will help you avoid the small-business lending trap set by your bank. What trap do I mean? The trap wherein the bank charges you an extraordinarily high commercial interest rate and, in addition to business collateral, demands your home and personal property as additional security. You can't afford to lose your home so the bank can be over-collateralized. There are better options.

Private money, as mentioned above, can be found through your broker, accountant, or lawyer. Additionally, for a small-business loan you can contact venture-capital clubs or place an ad in the newspaper.

Private money likes a good return on small-business loans, which may make the borrowing slightly more expensive (but usually not above bank rates). On the other hand, some private lenders offer rates substantially below the market. Regardless, their terms are usually liberal, which may be more important than rate.

Of course, you don't have to use a straight-loan scenario. Stock and/or debentures can be used, which may limit the cost but escalate the lender's say in your business—a serious negative.

Again, that notwithstanding, I strongly recommend private money for almost any consumer or commercial loan, but urge attention to detail in structuring the relationship.

Venture capital can be found through accountants, lawyers, financial advisors, and bankers.

These institutional private lenders normally want a strong vested interest in a company. Therefore, they commonly use a debt/equity structuring, which you may find difficult to accept. However, they have deep pockets, and are a source that must be considered when looking for substantial monies. I cannot over-state the necessity of caution with this source!

Business development corporations (BD.C.s) are private cor-porations chartered by state governments for the sole purpose of making loans to small businesses.

They are flexible in terms and are often overlooked by many because few are aware that they exist. Check your phone directory, and/or call your state capital's information operator. They will be able to direct you, provided that your state licenses BD.C.s.

These are private companies, so don't become lax and become confused by their association with the state government. You're no safer here than with any other lender.

State venture-capital funds: Approximately half the states have capital funds for small businesses. They are especially interested in new ventures, due to the obvious benefits that accrue to the state everytime new jobs are created.

Call your state capital information operator to see if your state has such a program. If so, it will direct your call.

This is an excellent source for funds if you're eligible. The plan is generally administered through the state's Industrial Development Commission.

Incubators are organizations set up by any number of associations. They can be sponsored in whole or in part by colleges, nonprofit organizations, and so on.

They provide services more than money, including shared office space, secretarial pools, executive assistance, and answering services. As a company progresses, and no longer needs to share expenses, it moves to its own quarters.

While the principal function of incubators is not to provide lending, on occasion they do have their own investment pools, out of which they will make loans under certain circumstances. Additionally, they have access to many other organizations that do provide lending, which may be the link you need.

Locating incubators can be difficult. Call your state university's information office. It will give you the number to contact.

Small Business Administration (SBA): The SBA is normally thought of as the court of last resort in the lending world. Meaning, it may make or assist with loans that no traditional lender will make. However, the SBA should be one of your first thoughts as opposed to the last.

I don't like to recommend doing business with any government agency for a variety of well-founded reasons. However, in this case, provided you can stand the extra time and paperwork involved, the bottom line may be profitable. The interest-rate saving, depending on the loan, may be substantial when applied to a large loan with extended terms. Then too, the terms can be extremely flexible. A bank funds the loan, but, since the SBA guarantees 90 percent of it, the bank's exposure to loss is minimal. Under those circumstances, favorable terms should be negotiable.

Suggestion: Shop your loan at institutions that have an SBA subdepartment in their loan department. Their sole purpose is to assist SBA applications. This will increase your chances of receiving approval, lessen your burden of paperwork, and perhaps offer options of which you are not currently aware.

For a listing of institutions that have SBA departments, call the local SBA office listed in your phone book.

Minority enterprise small-business investment corporations (MESBICs) are privately owned investment companies licensed by the Small Business Administration for the sole purpose of assisting minorities in acquiring financing for their new business ventures.

Call your local SBA office for the name and number of the nearest MESBIC.

Small-business investment companies (SBICs): These are privately owned investment companies licensed by the SBA for the sole purpose of assisting small businesses in acquiring lending for startup or operating.

Call your local SBA office for the name and number or location of SBICs in your area.

Using traditional lending sources may make finding money difficult, expensive, and risky to a small business. However, my experience is that, provided you have a viable business concept, there is money available from any one of a number of nontraditional sources. Clearly, with all the alternatives, the local financial institution loses much of its luster. And that's a good thing. Looking elsewhere will save you money, and perhaps your business and personal finances, which is why I've offered this listing.

Note: This alternative list and recommendations throughout the book should not be thought of as all-inclusive. These are the safer choices. If your needs are more sophisticated, you may wish to consider a Swiss bank account, offshore banking, private investments and so on.)

Is Your Bank Safe? Why You Should Care and How to Find Out
Most people don't care if their bank is safe. That's a mistake.

If your bank closes, at the very least you are going to be inconvenienced. Worse yet, as many customers have found out the hard way, you could lose a lot of money. If you don't understand the FDIC insurance limit and how it's now computed, you may fall over the limit and lose money you thought was insured. Probably the biggest risk is with your loans. When a bank closes, its loans are often put in the hands of liquidators. As many farmers and small businesses learned, again the hard way, liquidators will do almost anything to call a loan to get it off the books. If the customer can't pay, he or she often loses a farm, home, or business. This scenario happened again and again during the S&L crisis. It still happens almost daily, but to a lesser degree. As anyone who has gone through a bank closing can tell you, it can be a nightmare.

Even if your bank doesn't actually close, if it's not safe, you may pay a price. Like most businesses, when a bank's in trouble it usually means management is incompetent. The result is, you're continuing to trust most of your finances to a bank that doesn't deserve your trust. Then too, when a bank starts having profit trouble(s), it usually starts taking cost-cutting measures, reducing staff, and so on and that in turn leads to long teller lines, poor service across the board, reduction in the availability of loans, and so on. And, because the bank needs more income, service charges start going up even though service quality has gone down. So your bank doesn't have to close for you to pay a price for the fact that it is no longer safe. In short, everyone should know how safe their bank is. You wouldn't want to hire a lawyer who had been sued for malpractice twenty times, nor a doctor who was asked to leave three hospitals because he lost too many patients, or an accountant who had spent time in jail for embezzlement—so why should you continue banking at a bank that is within spitting distance of being closed? You shouldn't.

How can you determine the safety of your bank? It's rather simple.

First, check the local newspaper every quarter, as at that time every bank is required to publish a call report. Look in the "Capital" section and see if the bank's capital is enlarging every quarter. If so, the bank is showing a profit, which is a sign of stability. Also, check the "Loan Loss Reserve." If it is increasing along with the capital, it probably means it is not charging off too many loans—a sign of good asset management. Its deposits should be growing in a steady manner. No growth, or extremely rapid growth, normally is a sign of future difficulties.

For a more detailed review of your bank's condition, write to the FDIC, Disclosure Section, 1776 F Street NW, Room F518, Washington, D.C. 20429. Give the agency your bank's name and address, and specify what quarter's report you want (for example: third quarter 1995). For six dollars, the report you will receive is more than adequate to determine if your bank is having trouble, especially when you look in the loan section.

An even more in-depth, yet easy to read and understand, report about your bank or savings-and-loan association that also includes industry standards and comparisons can be obtained by contacting VERIBANC, Inc., P.O. Box 461, Wakefield, Massachusetts 01880; (800) 44BANKS (442-2657). Prices range from ten dollars to twenty-five dollars depending on the information requested. If you're in a hurry, VERIBANC offers an over-the-phone rating. For thirty-five dollars, you can order a "blue ribbon" report for the strongest banks in your area.

I cannot stress enough that you must make an effort to protect your accounts. The best way to accomplish this is to make sure you are banking with an institution that deserves your trust. Don't depend on the FDIC. Don't depend on the largeness of your bank for security, as a number of the nation's largest institutions are also among the least safe.

There are banks in every state that are too close to being closed. There are very small community banks that are in the same pitiful condition that some of the banking giants are. Protect yourself. Invest time and effort before you deposit a dime. Your bank's stability, or lack of it, must be known to you.

Glossary

Bankerese (banker double-talk) causes confusion. This glossary will help you better understand your choices and opportunities.

Administrator: An individual appointed by the court to settle the estate of someone who died without leaving a will.

Amortization Loans: A term that applies to long-term loans (like a mortgage) whereby the principal is paid off over the term of the loan, usually through monthly payments.

Annuity: A contract, usually with an insurance company, that pays a fixed amount of money at given times over a specified term.

Appraisal: The act of putting a value (fair market, sale, or loan value) on property (usually used in the context of real estate).

Appraiser: The person who performs the appraisal.

Appreciating Asset: An asset that increases in value with the passage of time: A house, in most instances, is one example.

Appreciation: The increase in the value of property as compared to its purchase price.

Arbitrage: The same-time sale of a purchased asset by a middleman called an arbitrager. The arbitrager's profit margin is the difference between the buy and sell price.

Asking Price: The price at which the owner of an asset offers to sell.

Asset: Anything of value.

Authorized Capital Stock: The number of shares of stock a company is legally authorized to issue.

Average Daily Balance: The daily balance of an account added together every day for thirty days and then divided by thirty. Used by financial institutions to ascertain profit and assess service charges.

Bad Debts: Those accounts of a company that are charged off due to delinquency or default.

Bag: A unit of measure. A bag of investment coins consists of any denomination of coin that totals one thousand dollars face value.

Balance of Payments: The total of any country's financial dealings with the rest of the world.

Balance Sheet: A corporate statement showing assets, liabilities, and capital.

Balloon Payment: A lump-sum payment due in the future. Normally, it is larger than the regular monthly payment. This type of payment is usually associated with mortgage lending.

Bank Account: Money deposited in a bank. Generally, these are checking or savings accounts.

Bank Holiday: A time span during which banks are legally permitted to deny withdrawal requests by their depositors. Usually associated with the Depression, but, on a state level, have occurred more than once recently (in Ohio, Maryland, Rhode Island).

Bankruptcy: A condition whereby an entity acknowledges that it cannot pay its debts. Further, liabilities exceed assets, so regardless of liquidation, a deficit still exists.

Banks: A corporation legally organized to provide deposit facilities to the public.

Bear Market: A period of time when the price trend of stocks, and/or other investment vehicles, is in a strong pattern of downward movement.

Bearer Instrument: Any ownership document that is payable to the "Bearer"; i.e., it indicates no specific party or payee. The owner is the person who is in possession.

Bearish: Believing a bear market is coming or is here.

Bid Price: The price a buyer is willing to pay for a purchase.

Beneficiary: The person for whose benefit a specific trust account operates.

Billion: A thousand millions.

Bond: A contractual agreement representing a loan for a specific amount and term. The party that buys the bond is the lender. The party selling the bond is the borrower. In most cases bonds are bought at face value, discount, or premium.

Book Value: The value of company stock as shown by the the institution's records. This is the company's total capital stock, capital surplus, undivided profits, and legal reserves divided by the number of outstanding shares.

Broker: A middleman for the stock market.

Bull Market: A period of time when the price trend of stocks, bonds, and so on, is in strong upward movement.

Bullion: Precious metals, usually in bar form.

Bullion Coin: An investment coin, sold for the value of its precious metal content as opposed to scarcity.

Bullish: Believing a bull market is coming or is here.

Call Loan: A loan that can be presented for payment at any time by the lender. Under most circumstances, a dangerous way to borrow money.

Call Option: The right to purchase a set quantity of stock or commodities at a given price if done so before a certain agreed-upon date.

Capital: The net assets of any corporation or person.

Capital and Surplus: A condensed accounting indicating a bank's financial strength. Comprised of a company's capital, surplus, undivided profits, and reserve accounts.

Capital Gain: A profit made from the sale of an investment.

Capital Stock: Stock that has been issued in return for payment of investment money from its shareholders.

Carrying Charges: The storing and/or interest charge on an investment.

Cash: A medium of exchange.

Cash Items: Deposited items given immediate credit but are subject to reversal against your account should they be returned for any reason.

Certificate of Deposit (CD): A receipt for a deposit payable either on demand or at a specific date in the future. Normally the CD is for a certain amount of money, at a certain interest rate, maturing at a specific date, and is a negotiable instrument.

Certified Check: A check that guarantees that the signature of the drawer is genuine and there are sufficient funds on deposit to insure payment. Payment cannot be denied.

Check: A negotiable instrument payable on demand.

Checking Account: An account against which checks may be drawn.

Collateral: An asset used to secure a loan. In case of default, the lender has the right to sell the asset to satisfy the debt.

Collateral Loan: A loan for which the borrower has pledged asset security.

Collateralized Assets: The assets pledged by the borrower for the purpose of meeting the security requirements as outlined by the lender.

Collected Balance: The balance in an account for which the bank has been paid for. The collected balance in an account is normally less than the actual balance.

Collection Items: Checks deposited in a bank for which the customer receives credit only when the item has been paid by the payee bank. This is accomplished through separate channels and not through normal clearing.

Common Stock: Common stock represents the last claim on assets.

Compensating Balances: Deposits in a checking account that a bank requires (to maximize its income) for approval on certain business loan applications. Usually 10 percent to 30 percent of the outstanding loan balance.

Content: The amount of precious metal in a bullion coin.

Convertible Currency: A currency that can be exchanged for an established commodity, usually a precious metal. The United States uses fiat money.

Convertible Security: A security that can be exchanged for another known security or commodity at the order of the owner.

Cost of Money: The interest rate one pays for the privilege of borrowing money.

Compound Interest: Interest paid on principal and accumulated (not withdrawn) interest previously earned.

Credit: As a liability, obtaining borrowed money. As an asset, a deposit to your account(s).

Currency: Government issued money.

Custodial Account: Any account whereby one individual holds the assets of another.

Cycle: Used in market terms, the recurring pattern of events.

Debit: Any form of withdrawal from your account(s).

Debenture: Bonds issued by a company that are not secured by any specific asset.

Defalcation: The illegal appropriation of money or property.

Default: The failure to meet the terms of a lending contract (i.e., nonpayment).

Deflation: A decrease in prices, usually caused by a reduction in the money supply.

Demand Deposits: Deposits subject to checks that can be withdrawn immediately (a checking account).

Demand Loan: A loan that is payable on demand by the lender. Another term for a call loan.

Deposits: Loans made by depositors to their financial institution.

Depreciation: The decrease in the value of property as compared to its cost.

Depression: Usually caused by a shortage of money or high-priced credit. Sometimes both are in evidence. This causes a reduction in the standard of living for the general population.

Devaluation: Lowering the redemption value of an asset. In general terms, this is usually an action taken by a government with regard to its currency.

Directors: The individuals who have the direct responsibility of corporate management.

Discount: The amount for which an asset is sold below its value.

Discount Rate: The interest rate charged commercial banks by the Federal Reserve for borrowed money.

Disinflation: A time span during which the inflation rate is in decline.

Dividend: A proportionate distribution/payment to shareholders of a company's earnings.

Downside Risk: The possible decline potential of an asset decreasing in value.

Draft: A negotiable instrument payable on acceptance, unlike a check, which is payable on demand.

Earned Income: Salary, wages, payment for services, and the like.

Earnings Per Share: The bank's yearly earnings divided by the number of shares of stock outstanding.

Economics: The study of how resources are used.

Embezzlement: The illegal appropriation of money.

Endorsement: The writing by the payee on the back of a negotiable instrument (usually a check). The signature passes title to another.

Equity: The net value of an asset. Its value minus its liabilities.

Exchange Control: Regulations restricting the export or import of specific currencies.

Exchange Rate: The value of one currency expressed in the value of another currency.

Executor: A person appointed through a will to carry out the financial wishes of the deceased.

Face Value: The value promised to a bondholder when the bond matures.

Federal Debt: The total amount of monies owed by the federal government to its creditors.

Federal Debt Limit: The limit of federal debt as allowed by law. This limit has no practical meaning anymore, as Congress simply increases it whenever it deems necessary. Instead of being the restraining vehicle it was intended to be, the debt limit has become a reminder of the inability of our legislators to control spending.

Federal Deficit: The yearly shortfalls between the money the government takes in and the money it spends. This difference is made up by additional borrowing, which then increases the problem through added debt service.

Federal Funds: Funds on deposit at the Federal Reserve Bank, made by member banks. This is the banking industry's daily investment pool.

Federal Reserve Bank: Any one of the twelve Federal Reserve banks.

Fiat Money: Money declared to be legal by a government. The currency is not convertible to gold, silver, and/or any other commodity. Its value is entirely based on trust.

Fiduciary: A person or corporation that is entrusted with the property of another.

Financial Statement: A balance sheet, or statement of condition. Can be prepared for business or personal use.

First Lien: The first claim right against a property, such as a home or other pledged security.

Fiscal Policy: The guidelines and policies that supposedly make up the monetary policy of a country. In effect it becomes the budgetary policy of the government.

Float: The funds deposited that receive immediate credit but have yet to be collected.

With the advent of deposit "hold time(s)," depositor float is virtually nonexistant. On the other hand, since the hold times are not consistant with actual collection times, bank float has become one of the bank's most profitable income-producers.

Foreclosure: Action taken by a lender when the conditions of the mortgage have not been met. The mortgage holder may institute proceedings to force the owner to pay the mortgage in full and/or sell the property. In a residence foreclosure the homeowner is normally alloted "redemption rights" for a minimum of one year. Additionally, even if a foreclosure is completed, in most states, the homeowner is allowed "homestead rights" of a specific dollar amount.

Forged Negotiable Instrument: Checks and other forms of payment that have had the maker's or payee's signature(s) falsified. Also applies to any document alteration for the purpose of defrauding.

Free Market: A market not regulated by government. Ours is referred to as a free market, but of course that's not the case.

Garnishment: A process authorizing a financial institution to impound monies on deposit for the purpose of paying another legal debt. The bank awaits a court order before forwarding any money.

Guarantee: A promise to pay in case of default of a lending debt.

Guarantor: A person who guarantees payment of a loan. The guarantor may or may not receive any benefit from the loan's proceeds.

Guardian: A person who has the legal right to control a minor and/or the estate of another.

Hold Time: The time limit a bank declares is necessary before it will allow a depositor to draw against funds he or she has deposited.

Holder in Due Course: A person who accepts a negotiable instrument for value, in good faith, and without prior knowledge that the instrument, a check for example, is defective in any way. A holder in due course is normally protected from any legal claims arising from dishonor or refusal to pay.

Inactive Account: A bank account that has little or no activity. These accounts are usually isolated from active accounts and then assessed monthly bank fees. Depending on the state laws, the bank will often remit the balance to the state revenue agency after the passage of five to ten years. The rightful owner of the account can always redeem the funds from the state by proving ownership.

Inflation: The devaluation of money. Usually caused by continual, uncontrolled private and government debt. In effect, it becomes a "tax" with which we can't keep pace. It has its most devastating effect on those who can afford it the least (i.e., the less affluent).

Installment Loan: A loan in which the borrower pays a portion of the value of the loan every month until the amount owed is completely repaid.

Insufficient Funds: The return of a check because the depositor does not have a sufficient balance to allow payment.

Interest: The "rental" cost of money paid by a bank to its savings depositors. Or, in a lending context, the "rental" cost of money paid by borrowers to a bank.

Interlocking Directors: Directors of one bank who are also directors of another bank or banks.

Joint Account: A bank account owned by two or more persons. Unless otherwise contracted, each has deposit and withdrawal rights.

Joint Tenancy: Property owned by two or more persons.

Junior Mortgage: A lower-ranking mortgage, as opposed to a first mortgage. There may be numerous junior mortgages on a property. Claims against the property are settled in order (i.e., first mortgage, second mortgage, third mortgage, and so on).

Kiting: The raising of nonexistent balances on uncollected funds among a number of financial institutions. Check kiting is a criminal offense.

Legal Tender: Any form of currency or money that legally must be accepted as payment for a debt.

Liabilities: The monetary obligations of a business or individual.

Lien: The right to hold property as a pledge against a loan, as in securing your auto loan with your car title. Or, as forced collateral for a legal obligation, as in the case of a mechanic's lien.

Line of Credit: The maximum prior-approved dollar amount that a specific person can borrow from his or her bank. In effect, a preapproved loan.

Liquid Assets: Current assets that can "immediately" be turned into cash.

Liquidation: The selling of an asset.

Loans: The renting of money, usually to be repaid with interest.

Lost Passbook: Since a passbook is only a memorandum of deposits, this is not a serious problem. A lost passbook should be reported to the bank immediately, however, to lessen your inconvenience and any loss to the bank.

Maker: A person who writes a check.

Market Value: The present salable value of a property.

Maturity: The due date of an obligation.

Million: A thousand thousands.

Minimum Free Balance: The minimum balance the bank requires in an account for that account to be free of a service fee.

Minutes: The written proceedings of a shareholder's or board of director's meeting.

Monetary Authority: The Constitution vested the power for creating money with Congress. It allows our representatives to create fiat money at their discretion. (The advisability of fiat money, and how the Congress uses its monetary authority, has long been debated. Historical results strongly indicate monetary abuse that has had a serious negative impact on our economy.)

Money: A medium of exchange.

Money Market: In an educational context, the supply of funds and the demand for said funds. In a general sense, another definition would be a "money market fund."

Mortgage: The document that conveys title to land that is used for collateral.

Negotiable Instrument: Orders to pay money. A check is a negotiable instrument.

Net Worth: The value of an estate or business after deducting all outstanding liabilities. A negative net worth exists when obligations exceed assets.

Note: A document indicating a debt and agreed upon promise to pay.

NSF: An abbreviation meaning nonsufficient funds.

Obligor: A person who owes money.

Overdraft: An account "on the books" of the bank that indicates the total balance of all accounts that are presently overdrawn.

On a specific account it indicates that the owner has paid out in excess of his or her deposits.

Overextension: A condition whereby a person has more debt than he or she can possibly be expected to repay.

Par Value: The face value of an instrument.

Passbook: A book that records bank deposits and withdrawals.

Payee: The person to whom a check is made payable.

Personal Check: A check written on the account of an individual as opposed to the account of a business.

Personal Property: All nonreal property owned by an individual.

Portfolio: All the investments, as expressed as a total, of a person or corporation.

Postdated Check: A check that bears a date in the future different from the date it was written.

Power of Attorney: A document that allows one individual to act on behalf of another. A power of attorney can be for a specific transaction or all legal transactions, depending on the intent of the grantor.

Prime Rate: The lending interest rate the banks charge their best commercial customers. (This is the banker's definition.)

Principal: The amount of a debt on which interest is computed.

Promissory Note: A note that indicates that a person or entity will pay a specified sum of money on a certain future date.

Purchasing Power: An expression of the value of money as it pertains to goods and services. Since fiat money has no intrinsic value, "purchasing power" is an important benchmark, as it assigns a "value" to the dollar.

Real Estate: Real property.

Recession: A decline in business activity. Usually caused by monetary shortages, it can sometimes be the prelude to the more severe problem of depression.

Refer to Maker: A method of returning a check that forces the payee to ask the maker why the check was not paid. It's the bank's way of avoiding involvement in the transaction, and/or not embarrassing the maker by sending the check back marked NSF.

Renewal: The extension of a loan by allowing the customer to "pay off" the old note with the proceeds of a new note.

Repurchase Agreement: A note sold by a bank, with the obligation/promise to repurchase it at a later date.

Returned Item: A check returned from the drawee bank to the presenting bank. There are varying reasons for returns, such as a missing endorsement, NSF, alterations, and postdated requirement.

Rule of 78s: The formula whereby a bank can accelerate consumer installment-loan interest into its profit accounts prior to when the interest is actually owed.

Savings Accounts: Funds on deposit at a bank that are not subject to check withdrawal and are paid interest.

Savings Banks: Banks that specialize in and promote savings by individuals.

Second Mortgage: A mortgage placed on property that already has a first mortgage.

Secured Loan: A loan where the borrower pledges collateral to the lender in case of default.

Security: Loan collateral.

Short-Term Loans: Loans that will mature within one year.

Sight Draft: A negotiable instrument payable on presentation (assuming all contractual aspects of the draft can be met).

Signatures: A bank is obligated by law to know the signatures of its depositors and is liable if it pays any negotiable instrument that has been forged on its customers' accounts.

Single-Payment Simple Interest Note: Unlike an installment loan in which interest is charged on the original balance throughout the term of the loan, single-payment simple interest notes charge the consumer interest only on the balance at any point in time.

This is the best loan vehicle for the average family to borrow money.

Speculation: An investment made solely on the anticipation of profits to be made from a change in price, as opposed to via dividends or interest returns. Speculation involves more than "normal" risk-taking.

Statement of Account: A record prepared by the bank and sent to the customer outlining all account transactions during a given month.

Stock Certificate: A certificate of ownership.

Stockholder: The owner of one or more shares of (bank) stock.

Stop Payment: The order to a bank not to honor a specific negotiable instrument. If the bank misses a stop payment order (assuming the order contained correct information and was presented soon enough to give the bank sufficient time to process it) it must reimburse the depositor for the amount of the check.

Tax: Property, usually currency, forcibly taken by a government. (The owner may be willing to pay the tax, but that point is moot, as the criterion for a tax is the ability to force compliance.)

Teller: A banker who accepts deposits and honors withdrawals.

Third Mortgage: A mortgage placed on property that already has a first and second lien on it.

Time Deposit: Deposits due a customer at a future date. This is a form of savings account and has many differing forms. Interest rates are based on the length of the contract between the customer and bank.

Title: Documented proof that a person or entity is the rightful owner of a specific piece of property.

Traveler's Checks: Prepaid checks sold by a bank that normally are honored worldwide. In many cases, the bank is just a middleman and the checks are actually drawn on a different corporation.

In addition to the fee involved, the corporation creates huge float for its own investment purposes, as the checks may take months to clear back to the account.

Treasury Bills: Noninterest-bearing, discounted notes issued by the U.S. Government. They are redeemed at face value.

Trillion: A thousand billions.

Trust: The supervision of property so an individual may benefit from the resulting income.

Trust Department: The bank department that transacts trust business.

Trustee: The person or entity to whom a trust is commended.

Unencumbered: Property free of all liability claims.

Unsecured Loan: A loan not having security (collateral).

U.S. Government Securities: Financial obligations of the U.S. Government. These can take many forms and are issued by many different government agencies and departments.

Usury: A loan interest rate in excess of the legal maximum.

Wealth: A measurement of usable resources.

Wire Transfer: The transfer of money verbally as opposed to by instrument. This is the fastest and safest way to get monies from one financial institution to another.

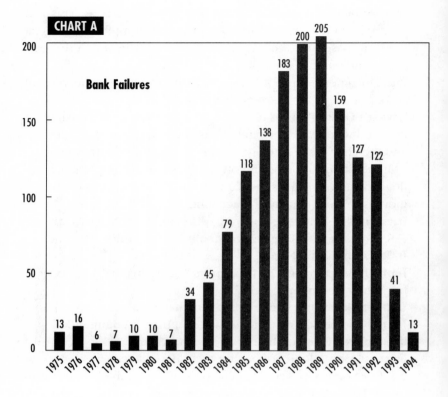

CHART A

Bank Failures

Year	
1975	13
1976	16
1977	6
1978	7
1979	10
1980	10
1981	7
1982	34
1983	45
1984	79
1985	118
1986	138
1987	183
1988	200
1989	205
1990	159
1991	127
1992	122
1993	41
1994	13

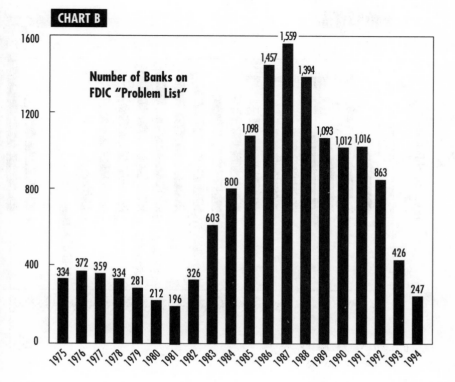

CHART B

Number of Banks on FDIC "Problem List"

Year	Value
1975	334
1976	372
1977	359
1978	334
1979	281
1980	212
1981	196
1982	326
1983	603
1984	800
1985	1,098
1986	1,457
1987	1,559
1988	1,394
1989	1,093
1990	1,012
1991	1,016
1992	863
1993	426
1994	247

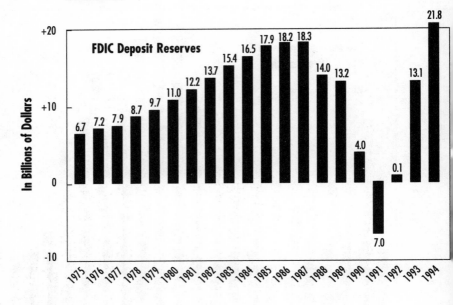

CHART C

FDIC Deposit Reserves

In Billions of Dollars

Year	Value
1975	6.7
1976	7.2
1977	7.9
1978	8.7
1979	9.7
1980	11.0
1981	12.2
1982	13.7
1983	15.4
1984	16.5
1985	17.9
1986	18.2
1987	18.3
1988	14.0
1989	13.2
1990	4.0
1991	7.0
1992	0.1
1993	13.1
1994	21.8

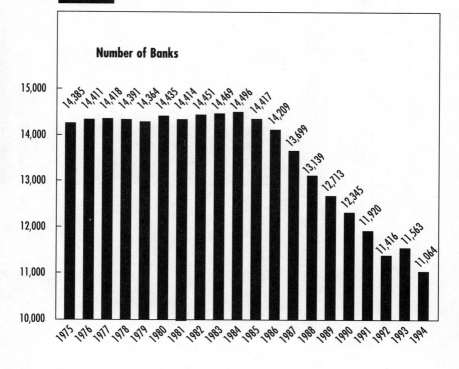

CHART D

Number of Banks